THE
FATHER'S
TOPICAL BIBLE

Tulsa, Oklahoma

Presented by
Wisdom International
P. O. Box 747
Dallas, Texas 75221
214/518-1833

Published by
Honor Books
P. O. Box 55388
Tulsa, Oklahoma 74155

10th Printing
Over 67,000 in Print

The Father's Topical Bible

All Scripture references are from
the *King James Version* of the Bible

ISBN 1-56292-021-9

Printed in the U.S.A.

Presented

to

_____

from

_____

_____

_____

Date

Additional copies of
The Father's Topical Bible
are available from your local bookstore
or by writing:

Honor Books • P.O. Box 35035 • Tulsa, OK 74153

Contents

Your Church

Your Personal Needs

THE SALVATION EXPERIENCE

There Are Three Basic Reasons To Believe the Bible Is the Infallible and Pure Word of God

1. No human would have written a standard this high. Think of the best person you know. You must admit he would have left certain Scriptures out had he written the Bible. So the Bible projects an inhuman standard and way of life. It has to be God because no man you know would have ever written a standard that high.

2. There is an aura, a climate, a charisma, a presence the Bible generates which no other book in the world creates. Lay an encyclopedia on your table at the restaurant – nobody will look at you twice. But when you lay your Bible on the table, they will stare at you, watch you chew your food, and even read your license plate when you get in your car! Why? The Bible creates the presence of God and forces a reaction in the hearts of men.

3. The nature of man is changed when he reads the Bible. Men change. Peace enters into their spirits. Joy wells up within their lives. Men like what they become when they read this book. Men accept Christ, because this Bible says Jesus Christ is the Son of God and that all have sinned and the wages of sin will bring death, and the only forgiveness that they can find is through Jesus, the Son of God.

Three Basic Reasons for Accepting Christ

1. *You needed forgiveness.* At some point in your life, you will want to be clean. You will hate guilt; you will crave purity. It's a built-in desire toward God, and you will have to address that appetite at some point in your life.

2. *You need a friend.* You may be sitting there saying, "But, don't I have friends?" Yes, but you have never had a friend like Jesus. Nobody can handle the information about your life as well as He can. He is the most consistent relationship you will ever know. Human friends vacillate in their reaction, depending on your mood or theirs. Jesus

Christ never changes his opinion of you. Nobody can tell Him anything which will change His mind about you. You cannot enjoy His world without His companionship.

3. *You needed a future.* All men have a built-in need for immortality, a craving for an eternity. God placed it within us. D.L. Moody once made a statement, "One of these days you are going to hear that I'm dead and gone. When you do, don't believe a word of it. I'll be more alive then, than at any other time in my life." Each of us wonders about eternity. What is death like? What happens when I die? Is there a hell? a heaven? a God? a devil? What happens? Every man wants to be around tomorrow. The only guarantee you will have of a future is to have the Eternal One on the inside of you. *He is Jesus Christ, the Son of God.*

The Gospel means Good News, you can change; your sins can be forgiven; your guilt can be dissolved; God loves *you.* He wants to be the difference in your life. "All have sinned and come short of the glory of God," Romans 3:23. "The wages of sin is death," Romans 6:23. You might say, what does that mean? It means that all unconfessed sin will be judged and penalized, but that is not the end of the story. The second part of verse 23 says "but the gift of God is eternal life through Jesus Christ our Lord." What does that mean? It means that between the wrath and judgment of God upon your sin, Jesus Christ, the Son of God, stepped in and absorbed your judgment and your penalty for you. God says if you recognize and respect Him and His worth as the Son of God, judgment will be withheld, and you will receive a pardon, forgiveness of all your mistakes.

What do you have to do? "If you believe in your heart that Jesus is the Son of God and that God raised him from the dead on the third day, and confess with your mouth, confession is made unto salvation, then you will be saved," Romans 10:9,10. What does the word "saved" mean? *Removed from danger.* It simply means if you respect and recognize the worth of Jesus Christ, God will take you out of the danger zone and receive you as a child of the Most High God. What is His gift that you are to receive? His Son. "For God so loved the world that he gave his only be-gotten Son, that whosoever believeth in Him should not perish but have everlasting life." John 3:16. How do you accept His Son?

Accept His mercy. How do you reject your sins? Confess them and turn away from them. "If I confess my sins he is faithful and just to forgive me my sins and to cleanse me from all unrighteousness." 1 John 1:9. That is the gospel.

YOUR RELATIONSHIP WITH GOD

Your Prayer Life

Seek the LORD and his strength, seek his face continually.

1 Chronicles 16:11

If my people, which are called by my name, shall humble themselves, and pray, and seek my face, and turn from their wicked ways; then will I hear from heaven, and will forgive their sin, and will heal their land.

2 Chronicles 7:14

When thou saidst, Seek ye my face; my heart said unto thee, Thy face, LORD, will I seek.

Psalms 27:8

Yet the LORD will command his loving-kindness in the daytime, and in the night his song shall be with me, and my prayer unto the God of my life.

Psalms 42:8

Seek the LORD, and his strength: seek his face evermore.

Psalms 105:4

Seek ye the LORD while he may be found, call ye upon him while he is near:

Isaiah 55:6

But thou, when thou prayest, enter into thy closet, and when thou hast shut thy door, pray to thy Father which is in secret; and thy Father which seeth in secret shall reward thee openly.

But when ye pray, use not vain repetitions, as the heathen do: for they think that they shall be heard for their much speaking.

Be not ye therefore like unto them: for your Father knoweth what things ye have need of, before ye ask him.

After this manner therefore pray ye: Our Father which art in heaven, Hallowed be thy name.

Matthew 6:6-9

And all things, whatsoever ye shall ask in prayer, believing, ye shall receive.

Matthew 21:22

Watch and pray, that ye enter not into temptation: the spirit indeed is willing, but the flesh is weak.

Matthew 26:41

And in the morning, rising up a great while before day, he went out, and departed into a solitary place, and there prayed.

Mark 1:35

Therefore I say unto you, What things soever ye desire, when ye pray, believe that ye receive them, and ye shall have them.

Mark 11:24

Take ye heed, watch and pray: for ye know not when the time is.

Mark 13:33

And he spake a parable unto them to this end, that men ought always to pray, and not to faint;

Luke 18:1

Watch ye therefore, and pray always, that ye may be accounted worthy to escape all these things that shall come to pass, and to stand before the Son of man.

Luke 21:36

Likewise the Spirit also helpeth our infirmities: for we know not what we should pray for as we ought: but the Spirit itself maketh intercession for us with groanings which cannot be uttered.

Romans 8:26

Rejoicing in hope; patient in tribulation; continuing instant in prayer;

Romans 12:12

Praying always with all prayer and supplication in the Spirit, and watching thereunto with all perseverance and supplication for all saints;

Ephesians 6:18

Be careful for nothing; but in every thing by prayer and supplication with thanksgiving let your requests be made known unto God.

Philippians 4:6

Continue in prayer, and watch in the same with thanksgiving;

Colossians 4:2

Pray without ceasing.

1 Thessalonians 5:17

I will therefore that men pray every where, lifting up holy hands, without wrath and doubting.

1 Timothy 2:8

Let us therefore come boldly unto the throne of grace, that we may obtain mercy, and find grace to help in time of need.

Hebrews 4:16

For the eyes of the Lord are over the righteous, and his ears are open unto their prayers: but the face of the Lord is against them that do evil.

1 Peter 3:12

But ye, beloved, building up yourselves on your most holy faith, praying in the Holy Ghost,

Jude 1:20

Your Study of God's Word

Ye shall not add unto the word which I command you, neither shall ye diminish ought from it, that ye may keep the commandments of the LORD your God which I command you.

Deuteronomy 4:2

And these words, which I command thee this day, shall be in thine heart:

Deuteronomy 6:6

The secret things belong unto the LORD our God: but those things which are revealed belong unto us and to our children for ever, that we may do all the words of this law.

Deuteronomy 29:29

But the word is very nigh unto thee, in thy mouth, and in thy heart, that thou mayest do it.

Deuteronomy 30:14

This book of the law shall not depart out of thy mouth; but thou shalt meditate therein day and night, that thou mayest observe to do according to all that is written therein: for then thou shalt make thy way prosperous, and then thou shalt have good success.

Joshua 1:8

Be ye mindful always of his covenant; the word which he commanded to a thousand generations;

1 Chronicles 16:15

Receive, I pray thee, the law from his mouth, and lay up his words in thine heart.

Job 22:22

Neither have I gone back from the commandment of his lips; I have esteemed the words of his mouth more than my necessary food.

Job 23:12

Blessed is the man that walketh not in the counsel of the ungodly, nor standeth in the way of sinners, nor sitteth in the seat of the scornful.

But his delight is in the law of the LORD; and in his law doth he meditate day and night.

Psalms 1:1,2

The law of the LORD is perfect, converting the soul: the testimony of the LORD is sure, making wise the simple.

Psalms 19:7

I will instruct thee and teach thee in the way which thou shalt go: I will guide thee with mine eye.

Psalms 32:8

The law of his God is in his heart; none of his steps shall slide.

Psalms 37:31

Wherewithal shall a young man cleanse his way? by taking heed thereto according to thy word.

Thy word have I hid in mine heart, that I might not sin against thee.

Thy word is a lamp unto my feet, and a light unto my path.

Psalms 119:9,11,105

When thou goest, it shall lead thee; when thou sleepest, it shall keep thee; and when thou awakest, it shall talk with thee.

For the commandment is a lamp; and the law is light; and reproofs of instruction are the way of life:

Proverbs 6:22,23

Commit thy works unto the LORD, and thy thoughts shall be established.

Proverbs 16:3

And thine ears shall hear a word behind thee, saying, This is the way, walk ye in it, when ye turn to the right hand, and when ye turn to the left.

Isaiah 30:21

The grass withereth, the flower fadeth: but the word of our God shall stand for ever.

Isaiah 40:8

Therefore whosoever heareth these sayings of mine, and doeth them, I will liken him unto a wise man, which built his house upon a rock:

Matthew 7:24

Jesus answered and said unto them, Ye do err, not knowing the scriptures, nor the power of God.

Matthew 22:29

Heaven and earth shall pass away: but my words shall not pass away.

Mark 13:31

Then said Jesus to those Jews which believed on him, If ye continue in my word, then are ye my disciples indeed;

And ye shall know the truth, and the truth shall make you free.

John 8:31,32

So then faith cometh by hearing, and hearing by the word of God.

Romans 10:17

All scripture is given by inspiration of God, and is profitable for doctrine, for reproof, for correction, for instruction in righteousness:

That the man of God may be perfect, throughly furnished unto all good works.

2 Timothy 3:16,17

Whereby are given unto us exceeding great and precious promises: that by these ye might be partakers of the divine nature, having escaped the corruption that is in the world through lust.

For the prophecy came not in old time by the will of man: but holy men of God spake as they were moved by the Holy Ghost.

2 Peter 1:4,21

Your Attitude Toward Praise and Worship

And they sang together by course in praising and giving thanks unto the LORD; because he is good, for his mercy endureth for ever toward Israel. And all the people shouted with a great shout, when they praised the LORD, because the foundation of the house of the LORD was laid.

Ezra 3:11

But as for me, I will come into thy house in the multitude of thy mercy: and in thy fear will I worship toward thy holy temple.

Psalms 5:7

I will give thee thanks in the great congregation: I will praise thee among much people.

Psalms 35:18

Blessed are they that dwell in thy house: they will be still praising thee.

Psalms 84:4

It is a good thing to give thanks unto the LORD, and to sing praises unto thy name, O most High:

To shew forth thy lovingkindness in the morning, and thy faithfulness every night,

Psalms 92:1,2

O come, let us worship and bow down: let us kneel before the LORD our maker.

Psalms 95:6

Make a joyful noise unto the LORD, all ye lands.

Serve the LORD with gladness: come before his presence with singing.

Know ye that the LORD he is God: it is he that hath made us, and not we ourselves; we are his people, and the sheep of his pasture.

Enter into his gates with thanksgiving, and into his courts with praise: be thankful unto him, and bless his name.

Psalms 100:1-4

Oh that men would praise the LORD for his goodness, and for his wonderful works to the children of men!

Let them exalt him also in the congregation of the people, and praise him in the assembly of the elders.

Psalms 107:8,32

I will worship toward thy holy temple, and praise thy name for thy lovingkindness and for thy truth: for thou hast magnified thy word above all thy name.

Psalms 138:2

Praise ye the LORD. Praise God in his sanctuary: praise him in the firmament of his power.

Praise him for his mighty acts: praise him according to his excellent greatness.

Praise him with the sound of the trumpet: praise him with the psaltery and harp.

Praise him with the timbrel and dance: praise him with stringed instruments and organs.

Praise him upon the loud cymbals: praise him upon the high sounding cymbals. Let every thing that hath breath praise the LORD. Praise ye the LORD.

Psalms 150: 1-3,5,6

Behold, God is my salvation; I will trust, and not be afraid: for the LORD JEHOVAH is my strength and my song; he also is become my salvation.

Isaiah 12:2

Sing, O ye heavens; for the LORD hath done it: shout, ye lower parts of the earth: break forth into singing, ye mountains, O forest, and every tree therein: for the LORD hath redeemed Jacob, and glorified himself in Israel.

Isaiah 44:23

Then saith Jesus unto him, Get thee hence, Satan: for it is written, Thou shalt worship the Lord thy God, and him only shalt thou serve.

Matthew 4:10

And Jesus answered and said unto him, Get thee behind me, Satan: for it is written, Thou shalt worship the Lord thy God, and him only shalt thou serve.

Luke 4:8

But the hour cometh, and now is, when the true worshippers shall worship the Father in spirit and in truth: for the Father seeketh such to worship him.

God is a Spirit: and they that worship him must worship him in spirit and in truth.

John 4:23,24

Now we know that God heareth not sinners: but if any man be a worshipper of God, and doeth his will, him he heareth.

John 9:31

What is it then? I will pray with the spirit, and I will pray with the understanding also: I will sing with the spirit, and I will sing with the understanding also.

1 Corinthians 14:15

For we are the circumcision, which worship God in the spirit, and rejoice in Christ Jesus, and have no confidence in the flesh.

Philippians 3:3

Continue in prayer, and watch in the same with thanksgiving;

Colossians 4:2

I will therefore that men pray every where, lifting up holy hands, without wrath and doubting.

1 Timothy 2:8

Your Hourly Obedience

And it shall come to pass, if ye shall hearken diligently unto my commandments which I command you this day, to love the LORD your God, and to serve him with all your heart and with all your soul,

That I will give you the rain of your land in his due season, the first rain and the latter rain, that thou mayest gather in thy corn, and thy wine, and thine oil.

Deuteronomy 11:13,14

But if thou shalt indeed obey his voice, and do all that I speak; then I will be an enemy unto thine enemies, and an adversary unto thine adversaries.

For mine Angel shall go before thee,

Exodus 23:22,23a

And if thou wilt walk in my ways, to keep my statutes and my commandments, as thy father David did walk, then I will lengthen thy days.

1 Kings 3:14

Blessed is the man that walketh not in the counsel of the ungodly, nor standeth in the way of sinners, nor sitteth in the seat of the scornful.

But his delight is in the law of the LORD; and in his law doth he meditate day and night.

Psalms 1:1,2

All the paths of the LORD are mercy and truth unto such as keep his covenant and his testimonies.

Psalms 25:10

The fear of the LORD is the beginning of wisdom: a good understanding have all they that do his commandments: his praise endureth for ever.

Psalms 111:10

Blessed are they that keep his testimonies, and that seek him with the whole heart.

Thou hast commanded us to keep thy precepts diligently.

Psalms 119:2,4

Keep my commandments, and live; and my law as the apple of thine eye.

Proverbs 7:2

He that keepeth the commandment keepeth his own soul; but he that despiseth his ways shall die.

Proverbs 19:16

If ye be willing and obedient, ye shall eat the good of the land:

Isaiah 1:19

Whosoever therefore shall break one of these least commandments, and shall teach men so, he shall be called the least in the kingdom of heaven: but whosoever shall do

and teach them, the same shall be called great in the kingdom of heaven.
Matthew 5:19

For whosoever shall do the will of my Father which is in heaven, the same is my brother, and sister, and mother.
Matthew 12:50

He that is faithful in that which is least is faithful also in much: and he that is unjust in the least is unjust also in much.

If therefore ye have not been faithful in the unrighteous mammon, who will commit to your trust the true riches?

And if ye have not been faithful in that which is another man's, who shall give you that which is your own?
Luke 16:10-12

If ye love me, keep my commandments.

Jesus answered and said unto him, If a man love me, he will keep my words: and my Father will love him, and we will come unto him, and make our abode with him.
John 14:15,23

If ye keep my commandments, ye shall abide in my love; even as I have kept my Father's commandments, and abide in his love.

Ye are my friends, if ye do whatsoever I command you.

John 15:10,14

Then Peter and the other apostles answered and said, We ought to obey God rather than men.

Acts 5:29

Though he were a Son, yet learned he obedience by the things which he suffered;

And being made perfect, he became the author of eternal salvation unto all them that obey him;

Hebrews 5:8-9

Submit yourselves therefore to God. Resist the devil, and he will flee from you. James 4:7

And whatsoever we ask, we receive of him, because we keep his commandments, and do those things that are pleasing in his sight.

And he that keepeth his commandments dwelleth in him, and he in him. And hereby we know that he abideth in us, by the Spirit which he hath given us.

1 John 3:22,24

YOUR ATTITUDE

The Loving Father

Hatred stirreth up strifes: but love covereth all sins.

Proverbs 10:12

Give to him that asketh thee, and from him that would borrow of thee turn not thou away.

Matthew 5:42

A new commandment I give unto you, That ye love one another; as I have loved you, that ye also love one another.

By this shall all men know that ye are my disciples, if ye have love one to another.

John 13:34,35

As the Father hath loved me, so have I loved you: continue ye in my love.

If ye keep my commandments, ye shall abide in my love; even as I have kept my Father's commandments, and abide in his love.

This is my commandment, That ye love one another, as I have loved you.

Greater love hath no man than this, that a man lay down his life for his friends.

Ye are my friends, if ye do whatsoever I command you.

Henceforth I call you not servants; for the servant knoweth not what his lord doeth: but I have called you friends; for all things that I have heard of my Father I have made known unto you.

Ye have not chosen me, but I have chosen you, and ordained you, that ye should go and bring forth fruit, and that your fruit should remain: that whatsoever ye shall ask of the Father in my name, he may give it you.

These things I command you, that ye love one another.

John 15:9,10,12-14,17

Owe no man any thing, but to love one another: for he that loveth another hath fulfilled the law.

Love worketh no ill to his neighbour: therefore love is the fulfilling of the law.

Romans 13:8,10

Though I speak with the tongues of men and of angels, and have not charity, I am become as sounding brass, or a tinkling cymbal.

And though I have the gift of prophecy, and understand all mysteries, and all knowledge; and though I have all faith, so that I could remove mountains, and have not charity, I am nothing.

And though I bestow all my goods to feed the poor, and though I give my body to be burned, and have not charity, it profiteth me nothing.

Charity suffereth long, and is kind; charity envieth not; charity vaunteth not itself, is not puffed up,

Doth not behave itself unseemly, seeketh not her own, is not easily provoked, thinketh no evil; Rejoiceth not in iniquity, but rejoiceth in the truth;

Beareth all things, believeth all things, hopeth all things, endureth all things.

Charity never faileth:

> *1 Corinthians 13:1-5,7-8a*

And now abideth faith, hope, charity, these three; but the greatest of these is charity.

> *1 Corinthians 13:13*

For this is the message that ye heard from the beginning, that we should love one another.

We know that we have passed from death unto life, because we love the brethren. He that loveth not his brother abideth in death.

My little children, let us not love in word, neither in tongue; but in deed and in truth.

> *1 John 3:11,14,18*

Beloved, let us love one another: for love is of God; and every one that loveth is born of God, and knoweth God.

He that loveth not knoweth not God; for God is love.

> *1 John 4:7,8*

The Understanding Father

I will bless the LORD, who hath given me counsel: my reins also instruct me in the night seasons.

Psalms 16:7

As for God, his way is perfect: the word of the LORD is tried: he is a buckler to all those that trust in him.

Psalms 18:30

Teach me thy way, O LORD, and lead me in a plain path, because of mine enemies.

Psalms 27:11

O send out thy light and thy truth: let them lead me; let them bring me unto thy holy hill, and to thy tabernacles.

Psalms 43:3

The LORD will perfect that which concerneth me: thy mercy, O LORD, endureth for ever: forsake not the works of thine own hands.

Psalms 138:8

Trust in the LORD with all thine heart; and lean not unto thine own understanding.

In all thy ways acknowledge him, and he shall direct thy paths.

Proverbs 3:5,6

Counsel is mine, and sound wisdom: I am understanding; I have strength.

Proverbs 8:14

Understanding is a wellspring of life unto him that hath it: but the instruction of fools is folly.

The heart of the wise teacheth his mouth, and addeth learning to his lips.

Proverbs 16:22,23

Through wisdom is an house builded; and by understanding it is established:

And by knowledge shall the chambers be filled with all precious and pleasant riches.

Proverbs 24:3,4

For my thoughts are not your thoughts, neither are your ways my ways, saith the LORD.

For as the heavens are higher than the earth, so are my ways higher than your ways, and my thoughts than your thoughts.

Isaiah 55:8,9

Call unto me, and I will answer thee, and shew thee great and mighty things, which thou knowest not.

Jeremiah 33:3

Then opened he their understanding, that they might understand the scriptures,

Luke 24:45

The Patient Father

Be ye strong therefore, and let not your hands be weak: for your work shall be rewarded.

2 Chronicles 15:7

Wait on the LORD: be of good courage, and he shall strengthen thine heart: wait, I say, on the LORD.

Psalms 27:14

Rest in the LORD, and wait patiently for him: fret not thyself because of him who prospereth in his way, because of the man who bringeth wicked devices to pass.

Psalms 37:7

I waited patiently for the LORD; and he inclined unto me, and heard my cry.

Psalms 40:1

For thou art my hope, O Lord GOD: thou art my trust from my youth.

Psalms 71:5

Better is the end of a thing than the beginning thereof: and the patient in spirit is better than the proud in spirit.

Be not hasty in thy spirit to be angry: for anger resteth in the bosom of fools.

Ecclesiastes 7:8,9

But they that wait upon the LORD shall renew their strength; they shall mount up with wings as eagles; they shall run, and not be weary; and they shall walk, and not faint.

Isaiah 40:31

Blessed is the man that trusteth in the LORD, and whose hope the LORD is.

Jeremiah 17:7

In your patience possess ye your souls.

Luke 21:19

And not only so, but we glory in tribulations also: knowing that tribulation worketh patience;

And patience, experience; and experience, hope:

And hope maketh not ashamed; because the love of God is shed abroad in our hearts by the Holy Ghost which is given unto us.

Romans 5:3-5

But if we hope for that we see not, then do we with patience wait for it.

Romans 8:25

For whatsoever things were written aforetime were written for our learning, that we through patience and comfort of the scriptures might have hope.

Now the God of patience and consolation grant you to be likeminded one toward another according to Christ Jesus:

Now the God of hope fill you with all joy and peace in believing, that ye may abound in hope, through the power of the Holy Ghost.

Romans 15:4,5,13

But the fruit of the Spirit is love, joy, peace, longsuffering, gentleness, goodness, faith,

Galatians 5:22

I can do all things through Christ which strengtheneth me.

Philippians 4:13

That ye be not slothful, but followers of them who through faith and patience inherit the promises.

Hebrews 6:12

Cast not away therefore your confidence, which hath great recompence of reward.

For ye have need of patience, that, after ye have done the will of God, ye might receive the promise.

For yet a little while, and he that shall come will come, and will not tarry.

Hebrews 10:35-37

Knowing this, that the trying of your faith worketh patience.

But let patience have her perfect work, that ye may be perfect and entire, wanting nothing.

James 1:3,4

Be patient therefore, brethren, unto the coming of the Lord. Behold, the husbandman waiteth for the precious fruit of the earth, and hath long patience for it, until he receive the early and latter rain.

Be ye also patient; stablish your hearts: for the coming of the Lord draweth nigh.

James 5:7,8

The Self-Controlled Father

Now therefore go, and I will be with thy mouth, and teach thee what thou shalt say.

Exodus 4:12

Teach me, and I will hold my tongue: and cause me to understand wherein I have erred.

Job 6:24

Who can understand his errors? cleanse thou me from secret faults.

Psalms 19:12

If ye be willing and obedient, ye shall eat the good of the land:

But if ye refuse and rebel, ye shall be devoured with the sword: for the mouth of the LORD hath spoken it.

Isaiah 1:19,20

For the Lord GOD will help me; therefore shall I not be confounded: therefore have I set my face like a flint, and I know that I shall not be ashamed.

Isaiah 50:7

The glory of this latter house shall be greater than of the former, saith the LORD of hosts: and in this place will I give peace, saith the LORD of hosts.

Haggai 2:9

For out of the abundance of the heart the mouth speaketh.

A good man out of the good treasure of the heart bringeth forth good things: and an evil man out of the evil treasure bringeth forth evil things.

But I say unto you, That every idle word that men shall speak, they shall give account thereof in the day of judgment.

For by thy words thou shalt be justified, and by thy words thou shalt be condemned.

Matthew 12:34b, 36,37

Verily I say unto you, Whatsoever ye shall bind on earth shall be bound in heaven: and whatsoever ye shall loose on earth shall be loosed in heaven.

Matthew 18:18

And he said, He that shewed mercy on him. Then said Jesus unto him, Go, and do thou likewise.

Luke 10:37

Servants, be obedient to them that are your masters according to the flesh, with fear and trembling, in singleness of your heart, as unto Christ;

With good will doing service, as to the Lord, and not to men:

Ephesians 6:5,7

Wherefore gird up the loins of your mind, be sober, and hope to the end for the grace that is to be brought unto you at the revelation of Jesus Christ;

As obedient children, not fashioning yourselves according to the former lusts in your ignorance:

1 Peter 1:13,14

Submit yourselves to every ordinance of man for the Lord's sake: whether it be to the king, as supreme;

Or unto governors, as unto them that are sent by him for the punishment of evildoers, and for the praise of them that do well.

For so is the will of God, that with well doing ye may put to silence the ignorance of foolish men:

1 Peter 2:13-15

Ye are of God, little children, and have overcome them: because greater is he that is in you, than he that is in the world.

We are of God: he that knoweth God heareth us; he that is not of God heareth not us. Hereby know we the spirit of truth, and the spirit of error.

And we have known and believed the love that God hath to us. God is love; and he that dwelleth in love dwelleth in God, and God in him.

Herein is our love made perfect, that we may have boldness in the day of judgment: because as he is, so are we in this world.

1 John 4:4,6,16-17

The Listening Father

The heart of the prudent getteth knowledge; and the ear of the wise seeketh knowledge.

Proverbs 18:15

Wherefore hear the word of the LORD, ye scornful men, that rule this people which is in Jerusalem.

Isaiah 28:14

And the man said unto me, Son of man, behold with thine eyes, and hear with thine ears, and set thine heart upon all that I shall shew thee;

Ezekiel 40:4a

And every one that heareth these sayings of mine, and doeth them not, shall be likened unto a foolish man, which built his house upon the sand:

And the rain descended, and the floods came, and the winds blew, and beat upon that house; and it fell: and great was the fall of it.

Matthew 7:26,27

But blessed are your eyes, for they see: and your ears, for they hear.

Matthew 13:16

Take heed therefore how ye hear: for whosoever hath, to him shall be given; and whosoever hath not, from him shall be taken even that which he seemeth to have.

Luke 8:18

He that is of God heareth God's words: ye therefore hear them not, because ye are not of God.

John 8:47

Pilate therefore said unto him, Art thou a king then? Jesus answered, Thou sayest that I am a king. To this end was I born, and for this cause came I into the world, that I should bear witness unto the truth. Every one that is of the truth heareth my voice.

John 18:37

But be ye doers of the word, and not hearers only, deceiving your own selves.

For if any be a hearer of the word, and not a doer, he is like unto a man beholding his natural face in a glass:

But whoso looketh into the perfect law of liberty, and continueth therein, he being not a forgetful hearer, but a doer of the work, this man shall be blessed in his deed.

James 1:22,23,25

He that hath an ear, let him hear what the Spirit saith unto the churches.

Revelation 2:29

The Teaching Father

Now therefore go, and I will be with thy mouth, and teach thee what thou shalt say.

Exodus 4:12

Teach me, and I will hold my tongue: and cause me to understand wherein I have erred.

Job 6:24

Shew me thy ways, O LORD; teach me thy paths.

Lead me in thy truth, and teach me: for thou art the God of my salvation; on thee do I wait all the day.

The meek will he guide in judgment: and the meek will he teach his way.

What man is he that feareth the LORD? him shall he teach in the way that he shall choose.

Psalms 25:4,5,9,12

Teach me thy way, O LORD, and lead me in a plain path, because of mine enemies.

Psalms 27:11

I will instruct thee and teach thee in the way which thou shalt go: I will guide thee with mine eye.

Psalms 32:8

I have declared my ways, and thou heardest me: teach me thy statutes.

Make me to understand the way of thy precepts: so shall I talk of thy wondrous works.

Psalms 119:26,27

Teach me to do thy will; for thou art my God: thy spirit is good; lead me into the land of uprightness.

Psalms 143:10

He that walketh with wise men shall be wise: but a companion of fools shall be destroyed.

Proverbs 13:20

When the scorner is punished, the simple is made wise: and when the wise is instructed, he receiveth knowledge.

Proverbs 21:11

O LORD, I know that the way of man is not in himself: it is not in man that walketh to direct his steps.

Jeremiah 10:24

Call unto me, and I will answer thee, and shew thee great and mighty things, which thou knowest not.

Jeremiah 33:3

And he said unto them, Unto you it is given to know the mystery of the kingdom of God: but unto them that are without, all these things are done in parables:

Mark 4:11

For I have given you an example, that ye should do as I have done to you.

John 13:15

Be ye therefore followers of God, as dear children;

And walk in love, as Christ also hath loved us, and hath given himself for us an offering and a sacrifice to God for a sweetsmelling savour.

Ephesians 5:1,2

Knowing that whatsoever good thing any man doeth, the same shall he receive of the Lord, whether he be bond or free.

Ephesians 6:8

For this cause also thank we God without ceasing, because, when ye received the word of God which ye heard of us, ye received it not as the word of men, but as it is in truth, the word of God, which effectually worketh also in you that believe.

1 Thessalonians 2:13

For when for the time ye ought to be teachers, ye have need that one teach you again which be the first principles of the oracles of God; and are become such as have need of milk, and not of strong meat.

For every one that useth milk is un-skillful in the word of righteousness: for he is a babe.

Hebrews 5:12,13

He that saith he abideth in him ought himself also so to walk, even as he walked.

1 John 2:6

The Approachable Father

The law of the LORD is perfect, con-verting the soul: the testimony of the LORD is sure, making wise the simple.

The statutes of the LORD are right, rejoicing the heart: the commandment of the LORD is pure, enlightening the eyes.

The fear of the LORD is clean, en-during for ever: the judgments of the LORD are true and righteous altogether.

More to be desired are they than gold, yea, than much fine gold: sweeter also than honey and the honeycomb.

Let the words of my mouth, and the meditation of my heart, be acceptable in thy sight, O LORD, my strength, and my redeemer.

Psalms 19:7-10,14

Lead me in thy truth, and teach me: for thou art the God of my salvation; on thee do I wait all the day.

The meek will he guide in judgment: and the meek will he teach his way.

Psalms 25:5,9

Teach me thy way, O LORD, and lead me in a plain path,

Psalms 27:11a

Trust in him at all times; ye people, pour out your heart before him: God is a refuge for us.

Psalms 62:8

Thou shalt guide me with thy counsel, and afterward receive me to glory.

Psalms 73:24

Then shalt thou call, and the LORD shall answer; thou shalt cry, and he shall say, Here I am. If thou take away from the midst of thee the yoke, the putting forth of the finger, and speaking vanity;

And if thou draw out thy soul to the hungry, and satisfy the afflicted soul; then shall thy light rise in obscurity, and thy darkness be as the noon day:

And the LORD shall guide thee continually, and satisfy thy soul in drought, and make fat thy bones: and thou shalt be like a watered garden, and like a spring of water, whose waters fail not.

Isaiah 58:9-11

The spirit of the Lord GOD is upon me; because the LORD hath anointed me to preach good tidings unto the meek; he hath sent me to bind up the brokenhearted, to proclaim liberty to the captives, and the opening of the prison to them that are bound;

But ye shall be named the Priests of the LORD: men shall call you the Ministers of our God: ye shall eat the riches of the Gentiles, and in their glory shall ye boast yourselves.

Isaiah 61:1,6

Ye are the salt of the earth: but if the salt have lost his savour, wherewith shall it be salted? it is thenceforth good for nothing, but to be cast out, and to be trodden under foot of men.

Ye are the light of the world. A city that is set on an hill cannot be hid.

Neither do men light a candle, and put it under a bushel, but on a candlestick; and it giveth light unto all that are in the house.

Let your light so shine before men, that they may see your good works, and glorify your Father which is in heaven.

Matthew 5:13-16

For I was an hungred, and ye gave me meat: I was thirsty, and ye gave me drink: I was a stranger, and ye took me in

Naked, and ye clothed me: I was sick, and ye visited me: I was in prison, and ye came unto me.

Then shall the righteous answer him, saying, Lord, when saw we thee an hungred, and fed thee? or thirsty, and gave thee drink?

When saw we thee a stranger, and took thee in? or naked, and clothed thee?

Or when saw we thee sick, or in prison, and came unto thee?

And the King shall answer and say unto them, Verily I say unto you, Inasmuch as ye have done it unto one of the least of these my brethren, ye have done it unto me.

Matthew 25:35-40

And he said unto them, Go ye into all the world, and preach the gospel to every creature.

Mark 16:15

But ye shall receive power, after that the Holy Ghost is come upon you: and ye shall be witnesses unto me both in Jerusalem, and in all Judaea, and in Samaria, and unto the uttermost part of the earth.

Acts 1:8

The Godly Father

He that walketh with wise men shall be wise: but a companion of fools shall be destroyed.

Proverbs 13:20

And whosoever shall give to drink unto one of these little ones a cup of cold water only in the name of a disciple, verily I say unto you, he shall in no wise lose his reward.

Matthew 10:42

Even as the Son of man came not to be ministered unto, but to minister, and to give his life a ransom for many.

Matthew 20:28

But so shall it not be among you: but whosoever will be great among you, shall be your minister:

And whosoever of you will be the chiefest, shall be servant of all.

Mark 10:43,44

And he said, He that shewed mercy on him. Then said Jesus unto him, Go, and do thou likewise.

Luke 10:37

Verily, verily, I say unto you, The servant is not greater than his lord; neither he that is sent greater than he that sent him.

A new commandment I give unto you, That ye love one another; as I have loved you, that ye also love one another.

John 13:16,34

Now the God of patience and consolation grant you to be likeminded one toward another according to Christ Jesus:

That ye may with one mind and one mouth glorify God, even the Father of our Lord Jesus Christ.

Wherefore receive ye one another, as Christ also received us to the glory of God.
Romans 15:5-7

Moreover it is required in stewards, that a man be found faithful.
1 Corinthians 4:2

Therefore, my beloved brethren, be ye stedfast, unmoveable, always abounding in the work of the Lord, forasmuch as ye know that your labour is not in vain in the Lord.
1 Corinthians 15:58

Bear ye one another's burdens, and so fulfil the law of Christ.

As we have therefore opportunity, let us do good unto all men, especially unto them who are of the household of faith.
Galatians 6:2,10

Be ye therefore followers of God, as dear children;

And walk in love, as Christ also hath loved us, and hath given himself for us an offering and a sacrifice to God for a sweetsmelling savour.

Ephesians 5:1,2

Servants, be obedient to them that are your masters according to the flesh, with fear and trembling, in singleness of your heart, as unto Christ;

With good will doing service, as to the Lord, and not to men:

Ephesians 6:5,7

Let this mind be in you, which was also in Christ Jesus:

Who, being in the form of God, thought it not robbery to be equal with God:

But made himself of no reputation, and took upon him the form of a servant, and was made in the likeness of men:

And being found in fashion as a man, he humbled himself, and became obedient unto death, even the death of the cross.

Philippians 2:5-8

Forbearing one another, and forgiving one another, if any man have a quarrel against any: even as Christ forgave you, so also do ye.

Servants, obey in all things your masters according to the flesh; not with eyeservice, as menpleasers; but in singleness of heart, fearing God:

Colossians 3:13,22

Looking unto Jesus the author and finisher of our faith; who for the joy that was set before him endured the cross, despising the shame, and is set down at the right hand of the throne of God.

For consider him that endured such contradiction of sinners against himself, lest ye be wearied and faint in your minds.

Hebrews 12:2,3

For even hereunto were ye called: because Christ also suffered for us, leaving us an example, that ye should follow his steps:

1 Peter 2:21

The Father of Integrity

Let me be weighed in an even balance that God may know mine integrity.

Job 31:6

Blessed is the man that walketh not in the counsel of the ungodly, nor standeth in the way of sinners, nor sitteth in the seat of the scornful.

But his delight is in the law of the LORD; and in his law doth he meditate day and night.

Psalms 1:1,2

All the paths of the LORD are mercy and truth unto such as keep his covenant and his testimonies.

Let integrity and uprightness preserve me; for I wait on thee.

Psalms 25:10,

Judge me, O LORD; for I have walked in mine integrity: I have trusted also in the LORD; therefore I shall not slide.

Psalms 26:1

And as for me, thou upholdest me in mine integrity, and settest me before thy face for ever.

Psalms 41:12

So he fed them according to the integrity of his heart; and guided them by the skilfulness of his hands.

Psalms 78:72

The fear of the LORD is the beginning of wisdom: a good understanding have all they that do his commandments: his praise endureth for ever.

Psalms 111:10

Blessed are they that keep his testimonies, and that seek him with the whole heart.

Thou hast commanded us to keep thy precepts diligently.

Psalms 119:2,4

The integrity of the upright shall guide them: but the perverseness of transgressors shall destroy them.

Proverbs 11:3

Better is the poor that walketh in his integrity, than he that is perverse in his lips, and is a fool.

He that keepeth the commandment keepeth his own soul; but he that despiseth his ways shall die.

Proverbs 19:1,16

The just man walketh in his integrity: his children are blessed after him.

Proverbs 20:7

If ye be willing and obedient, ye shall eat the good of the land:

Isaiah 1:19

Recompense to no man evil for evil. Provide things honest in the sight of all men.

Romans 12:17

Finally, brethren, whatsoever things are true, whatsoever things are honest, whatsoever things are just, whatsoever things are pure, whatsoever things are lovely, whatsoever things are of good report; if there be any virtue, and if there be any praise, think on these things.

Philippians 4:8

The Father Who Is a Leader

And if thou wilt walk before me, as David thy father walked, in integrity of heart, and in uprightness, to do according to all that I have commanded thee, and wilt keep my statutes and my judgments:

Then I will establish the throne of thy kingdom upon Israel for ever, as I promised to David thy father, saying, There shall not fail thee a man upon the throne of Israel.

1 Kings 9:4,5

The steps of a good man are ordered by the LORD: and he delighteth in his way.

Psalms 37:23

For the LORD God is a sun and shield: the LORD will give grace and glory: no good thing will he withhold from them that walk uprightly.

Psalms 84:11

A good man sheweth favour, and lendeth: he will guide his affairs with discretion.

Psalms 112:5

Better is a little with righteousness than great revenues without right.

A man's heart deviseth his way: but the LORD directeth his steps.

Proverbs 16:8,9

A false balance is abomination to the LORD: but a just weight is his delight.

Proverbs 11:1

And thine ears shall hear a word behind thee, saying, This is the way, walk ye in it, when ye turn to the right hand, and when ye turn to the left.

Isaiah 30:21

Thus speaketh the LORD of hosts, saying, Execute true judgment, and shew mercy and compassions every man to his brother:

And oppress not the widow, nor the fatherless, the stranger, nor the poor; and let none of you imagine evil against his brother in your heart.

Zechariah 7:9,10

For with what judgment ye judge, ye shall be judged: and with what measure ye mete, it shall be measured to you again.

Matthew 7:2

Howbeit when he, the Spirit of truth, is come, he will guide you into all truth: for he shall not speak of himself; but whatsoever he shall hear, that shall he speak: and he will shew you things to come.

John 16:13

Then Peter and the other apostles answered and said, We ought to obey God rather than men.

Acts 5:29

For as many as are led by the Spirit of God, they are the sons of God.

Romans 8:14

For kings, and for all that are in authority; that we may lead a quiet and peaceable life in all godliness and honesty.

1 Timothy 2:2

Submit yourselves to every ordinance of man for the Lord's sake: whether it be to the king, as supreme;

Or unto governors, as unto them that are sent by him for the punishment of evildoers, and for the praise of them that do well.

For so is the will of God, that with well doing ye may put to silence the ignorance of foolish men:

1 Peter 2:13-15

The Disciplinarian Father

Shew me thy ways, O LORD; teach me thy paths.

What man is he that feareth the LORD? him shall he teach in the way that he shall choose.

Psalms 25:4,12

Teach me thy way, O LORD, and lead me in a plain path, because of mine enemies.

I had fainted, unless I had believed to see the goodness of the LORD in the land of the living.

Wait on the LORD: be of good courage, and he shall strengthen thine heart: wait, I say, on the LORD.

Psalms 27:11,13,14

The LORD is my strength and my shield; my heart trusted in him, and I am helped: therefore my heart greatly rejoiceth; and with my song will I praise him.

Psalms 28:7

Cast thy burden upon the LORD, and he shall sustain thee: he shall never suffer the righteous to be moved.

Psalms 55:22

Though I walk in the midst of trouble, thou wilt revive me: thou shalt stretch forth thine hand against the wrath of mine enemies, and thy right hand shall save me.

Psalms 138:7

Teach me to do thy will; for thou art my God: thy spirit is good; lead me into the land of uprightness.

Psalms 143:10

Keep my commandments, and live; and my law as the apple of thine eye.

Proverbs 7:2

Answer not a fool according to his folly, lest thou also be like unto him.

Proverbs 26:4

If ye be willing and obedient, ye shall eat the good of the land:

But if ye refuse and rebel, ye shall be devoured with the sword: for the mouth of the LORD hath spoken it.

Isaiah 1:19,20

O LORD, correct me, but with judgment; not in thine anger, lest thou bring me to nothing.

Jeremiah 10:24

And he said, He that shewed mercy on him. Then said Jesus unto him, Go, and do thou likewise.

Luke 10:37

Then Peter and the other apostles answered and said, We ought to obey God rather than men.

Acts 5:29

Servants, be obedient to them that are your masters according to the flesh, with fear and trembling, in singleness of your heart, as unto Christ;

With good will doing service, as to the Lord, and not to men:

Ephesians 6:5,7

Wherefore gird up the loins of your mind, be sober, and hope to the end for the grace that is to be brought unto you at the revelation of Jesus Christ;

As obedient children, not fashioning yourselves according to the former lusts in your ignorance:

1 Peter 1:13,14

The Motivating Father

The LORD shall cause thine enemies that rise up against thee to be smitten before thy face: they shall come out against thee one way, and flee before thee seven ways.

Deuteronomy 28:7

Be strong and of a good courage, fear not, nor be afraid of them: for the LORD thy God, he it is that doth go with thee; he will not fail thee, nor forsake thee.

Deuteronomy 31:6

Moreover as for me, God forbid that I should sin against the LORD in ceasing to pray for you: but I will teach you the good and the right way:

1 Samuel 12:23

And he answered, Fear not: for they that be with us are more than they that be with them.

2 Kings 6:16

Through thee will we push down our enemies: through thy name will we tread them under that rise up against us.

Psalms 44:5

It is better to hear the rebuke of the wise, than for a man to hear the song of fools.

Ecclesiastes 7:5

For I the LORD thy God will hold thy right hand, saying unto thee, Fear not; I will help thee.

Isaiah 41:13

The spirit of the Lord GOD is upon me; because the LORD hath anointed me to preach good tidings unto the meek; he hath sent me to bind up the brokenhearted, to proclaim liberty to the captives, and the opening of the prison to them that are bound;

Isaiah 61:1

And they that be wise shall shine as the brightness of the firmament; and they that turn many to righteousness as the stars for ever and ever.

Daniel 12:3

Ask, and it shall be given you; seek, and ye shall find; knock, and it shall be opened unto you:

For every one that asketh receiveth; and he that seeketh findeth; and to him that knocketh it shall be opened.

Matthew 7:7,8

And ye shall know the truth, and the truth shall make you free. If the Son therefore shall make you free, ye shall be free indeed.

John 8:32,36

Verily, verily, I say unto you, He that believeth on me, the works that I do shall he do also; and greater works than these shall he do; because I go unto my Father.

John 14:12

But ye shall receive power, after that the Holy Ghost is come upon you: and ye shall be witnesses unto me both in Jerusalem, and in all Judaea, and in Samaria, and unto the uttermost part of the earth.

Acts 1:8

For the weapons of our warfare are not carnal, but mighty through God to the pulling down of strong holds; 2 Corinthians 10:4

Wherefore he saith, Awake thou that sleepest, and arise from the dead, and Christ shall give thee light.

Ephesians 5:14

I can do all things through Christ which strengtheneth me.

Philippians 4:13

Strengthened with all might, according to his glorious power, unto all patience and longsuffering with joyfulness;

Colossians 1:11

Walk in wisdom toward them that are without, redeeming the time.

Colossians 4:5

Wherefore I put thee in remembrance that thou stir up the gift of God, which is in thee by the putting on of my hands.

2 Timothy 1:6

Ye are of God, little children, and have overcome them: because greater is he that is in you, than he that is in the world.

We are of God: he that knoweth God heareth us; he that is not of God heareth not us. Hereby know we the spirit of truth, and the spirit of error.

And we have known and believed the love that God hath to us. God is love; and he that dwelleth in love dwelleth in God, and God in him. Herein is our love made perfect, that we may have boldness in the day of judgment: because as he is, so are we in this world.

1 John 4:4,6,16,17

The Providing Father

For thou art my rock and my fortress; therefore for thy name's sake lead me, and guide me.

Psalms 31:3

Trust in the LORD, and do good; so shalt thou dwell in the land, and verily thou shalt be fed.

Delight thyself also in the LORD; and he shall give thee the desires of thine heart.

Commit thy way unto the LORD; trust also in him; and he shall bring it to pass.

And he shall bring forth thy righteousness as the light, and thy judgment as the noonday.

For evildoers shall be cut off: but those that wait upon the LORD, they shall inherit the earth.

I have been young, and now am old; yet have I not seen the righteous forsaken, nor his seed begging bread.

For the LORD loveth judgment, and forsaketh not his saints; they are preserved for ever: but the seed of the wicked shall be cut off.

Psalms 37:3-6,9,25,28

For thou hast been a strength to the poor, a strength to the needy in his distress, a refuge from the storm, a shadow from the heat, when the blast of the terrible ones is as a storm against the wall.

Isaiah 25:4

I can do all things through Christ which strengtheneth me.

But my God shall supply all your need according to his riches in glory by Christ Jesus.

Philippians 4:13,19

If any of you lack wisdom, let him ask of God, that giveth to all men liberally, and upbraideth not; and it shall be given him.

James 1:5

But the wisdom that is from above is first pure, then peaceable, gentle, and easy to be intreated, full of mercy and good fruits, without partiality, and without hypocrisy.

And the fruit of righteousness is sown in peace of them that make peace.

James 3:17,18

The effectual fervent prayer of a righteous man availeth much.

James 5:16b

The Faithful Father

And it came to pass, as she spake to Joseph day by day, that he hearkened not unto her, to lie by her, or to be with her.

And it came to pass about this time, that Joseph went into the house to do his business; and there was none of the men of the house there within.

And she caught him by his garment, saying, Lie with me: and he left his garment in her hand, and fled, and got him out.

Genesis 39:10-12

My times are in thy hand: deliver me from the hand of mine enemies, and from them that persecute me.

Make thy face to shine upon thy servant: save me for thy mercies' sake.

Psalms 31:15,16

Thou art my hiding place; thou shalt preserve me from trouble; thou shalt compass me about with songs of deliverance.

Psalms 32:7

For the LORD shall be thy confidence,
Proverbs 3:26a

But they that wait upon the LORD shall renew their strength; they shall mount up with wings as eagles; they shall run, and not be weary; and they shall walk, and not faint.
Isaiah 40:31

Therefore all things whatsoever ye would that men should do to you, do ye even so to them: for this is the law and the prophets.
Matthew 7:12

Flee fornication. Every sin that a man doeth is without the body; but he that committeth fornication sinneth against his own body.
1 Corinthians 6:18

And be ye kind one to another, tenderhearted, forgiving one another, even as God for Christ's sake hath forgiven you.
Ephesians 4:32

Husbands, love your wives, even as Christ also loved the church, and gave himself for it;

That he might sanctify and cleanse it with the washing of water by the word,

That he might present it to himself a glorious church, not having spot, or wrinkle, or any such thing; but that it should be holy and without blemish.

So ought men to love their wives as their own bodies. He that loveth his wife loveth himself.

For no man ever yet hated his own flesh; but nourisheth and cherisheth it, even as the Lord the church:

For we are members of his body, of his flesh, and of his bones.

For this cause shall a man leave his father and mother, and shall be joined unto his wife, and they two shall be one flesh.

This is a great mystery: but I speak concerning Christ and the church.

Nevertheless let every one of you in particular so love his wife even as himself; and the wife see that she reverence her husband.

Ephesians 5:25-33

And the peace of God, which passeth all understanding, shall keep your hearts and minds through Christ Jesus.

Finally, brethren, whatsoever things are true, whatsoever things are honest, whatsoever things are just, whatsoever things are pure, whatsoever things are lovely, whatsoever things are of good report; if there be any virtue, and if there be any praise, think on these things.

Philippians 4:7,8

Not rendering evil for evil, or railing for railing: but contrariwise blessing; knowing that ye are thereunto called, that ye should inherit a blessing.

1 Peter 3:9

The Considerate Father

Cease from anger, and forsake wrath: fret not thyself in any wise to do evil.

Psalms 37:8

A good man sheweth favour, and lendeth: he will guide his affairs with discretion.

Psalms 112:5

A friend loveth at all times, and a brother is born for adversity.

Proverbs 17:17

He that hath pity upon the poor lendeth unto the LORD; and that which he hath given will he pay him again.

Proverbs 19:17

He that hath a bountiful eye shall be blessed; for he giveth of his bread to the poor.

Proverbs 22:9

He that giveth unto the poor shall not lack: but he that hideth his eyes shall have many a curse.

Proverbs 28:27

Therefore all things whatsoever ye would that men should do to you, do ye even so to them: for this is the law and the prophets.

Matthew 7:12

Give, and it shall be given unto you; good measure, pressed down, and shaken together, and running over, shall men give into your bosom. For with the same measure that ye mete withal it shall be measured to you again.

Luke 6:38

Upon the first day of the week let every one of you lay by him in store, as God hath prospered him, that there be no gatherings when I come.

1 Corinthians 16:2

But this I say, He which soweth sparingly shall reap also sparingly; and he which soweth bountifully shall reap also bountifully.

Every man according as he purposeth in his heart, so let him give; not grudgingly, or of necessity: for God loveth a cheerful giver.

And God is able to make all grace abound toward you; that ye, always having all sufficiency in all things, may abound to every good work:

2 Corinthians 9:6-8

Charge them that are rich in this world, that they be not highminded, nor trust in uncertain riches, but in the living God, who giveth us richly all things to enjoy;

That they do good, that they be rich in good works, ready to distribute, willing to communicate;

Laying up in store for themselves a good foundation against the time to come, that they may lay hold on eternal life.

1 Timothy 6:17-19

But whoso hath this world's good, and seeth his brother have need, and shutteth up his bowels of compassion from him, how dwelleth the love of God in him?

My little children, let us not love in word, neither in tongue; but in deed and in truth.

1 John 3:17,18

The Kind Father

Cease from anger, and forsake wrath: fret not thyself in any wise to do evil.

Psalms 37:8

A soft answer turneth away wrath: but grievous words stir up anger.

A wrathful man stirreth up strife: but he that is slow to anger appeaseth strife.

Proverbs 15:1,18

The desire of a man is his kindness: and a poor man is better than a liar.

Proverbs 19:22

He that hath my commandments, and keepeth them, he it is that loveth me: and he that loveth me shall be loved of my Father, and I will love him, and will manifest myself to him.

John 14:21

As the Father hath loved me, so have I loved you: continue ye in my love.

If ye keep my commandments, ye shall abide in my love; even as I have kept my Father's commandments, and abide in his love.

This is my commandment, That ye love one another, as I have loved you.

John 15:9,10,12

But in all things approving ourselves as the ministers of God, in much patience, in afflictions, in necessities, in distresses,

By pureness, by knowledge, by long-suffering, by kindness, by the Holy Ghost, by love unfeigned,

2 Corinthians 6:4,6

And let us not be weary in well doing: for in due season we shall reap, if we faint not.

Galatians 6:9

Let all bitterness, and wrath, and anger, and clamour, and evil speaking, be put away from you, with all malice:

And be ye kind one to another, tender-hearted, forgiving one another, even as God for Christ's sake hath forgiven you.

Ephesians 4:31,32

That ye might walk worthy of the Lord unto all pleasing, being fruitful in every good work, and increasing in the knowledge of God;

Colossians 1:10

Put on therefore, as the elect of God, holy and beloved, bowels of mercies, kindness, humbleness of mind, meekness, longsuffering;

Forbearing one another, and forgiving one another, if any man have a quarrel against any: even as Christ forgave you, so also do ye.

Colossians 3:12,13

And beside this, giving all diligence, add to your faith virtue; and to virtue knowledge;

And to knowledge temperance; and to temperance patience; and to patience godliness;

And to godliness brotherly kindness; and to brotherly kindness charity.

For if these things be in you, and abound, they make you that ye shall neither be barren nor unfruitful in the knowledge of our Lord Jesus Christ.

2 Peter 1:5-8

Beloved, let us love one another: for love is of God; and every one that loveth is born of God, and knoweth God.

He that loveth not knoweth not God; for God is love.

1 John 4:7,8

YOUR CHILD

When Your Child Becomes Rebellious Toward You

Now therefore go, and I will be with thy mouth, and teach thee what thou shalt say.

Exodus 4:12

Behold, to obey is better than sacrifice, and to hearken than the fat of rams.

For rebellion is as the sin of witchcraft, and stubbornness is as iniquity and idolatry. Because thou hast rejected the word of the LORD, he hath also rejected thee from being king.

1 Samuel 15:22b

Teach me, and I will hold my tongue: and cause me to understand wherein I have erred.

Job 6:24

Shew me thy ways, O LORD; teach me thy paths.

What man is he that feareth the LORD? him shall he teach in the way that he shall choose.

Psalms 25:4,12

I had fainted, unless I had believed to see the goodness of the LORD in the land of the living.

Wait on the LORD: be of good courage, and he shall strengthen thine heart: wait, I say, on the LORD.

Psalms 27:13,14

The LORD is my strength and my shield; my heart trusted in him, and I am helped: therefore my heart greatly rejoiceth; and with my song will I praise him.

Psalms 28:7

Cast thy burden upon the LORD, and he shall sustain thee: he shall never suffer the righteous to be moved.

Psalms 55:22

Though I walk in the midst of trouble, thou wilt revive me: thou shalt stretch forth thine hand against the wrath of mine enemies, and thy right hand shall save me.

Psalms 138:7

Teach me to do thy will; for thou art my God: thy spirit is good; lead me into the land of uprightness.

Psalms 143:10

Keep my commandments, and live; and my law as the apple of thine eye.

Proverbs 7:2

Answer not a fool according to his folly, lest thou also be like unto him.

Proverbs 26:4

If ye be willing and obedient, ye shall eat the good of the land:

But if ye refuse and rebel, ye shall be devoured with the sword: for the mouth of the LORD hath spoken it.

Isaiah 1:19,20

Can a woman forget her sucking child, that she should not have compassion on the son of her womb? yea, they may forget, yet will I not forget thee.

Isaiah 49:15

And I will give unto thee the keys of the kingdom of heaven: and whatsoever thou shalt bind on earth shall be bound in heaven: and whatsoever thou shalt loose on earth shall be loosed in heaven.

Matthew 16:19

And he called unto him the twelve, and began to send them forth by two and two; and gave them power over unclean spirits;

Mark 6:7

Behold, I give unto you power to tread on serpents and scorpions, and over all the power of the enemy: and nothing shall by any means hurt you.

Luke 10:19

Take heed to yourselves: If thy brother trespass against thee, rebuke him; and if he repent, forgive him.

Luke 17:3

Then Peter and the other apostles answered and said, We ought to obey God rather than men.

Acts 5:29

And, ye fathers, provoke not your children to wrath: but bring them up in the nurture and admonition of the Lord.

Servants, be obedient to them that are your masters according to the flesh, with fear and trembling, in singleness of your heart, as unto Christ;

With good will doing service, as to the Lord, and not to men:

Ephesians 6:4,5,7

Wherefore gird up the loins of your mind, be sober, and hope to the end for the grace that is to be brought unto you at the revelation of Jesus Christ;

As obedient children, not fashioning yourselves according to the former lusts in your ignorance:

1 Peter 1:13,14

Submit yourselves to every ordinance of man for the Lord's sake: whether it be to the king, as supreme;

Or unto governors, as unto them that are sent by him for the punishment of evildoers, and for the praise of them that do well.

For so is the will of God, that with well doing ye may put to silence the ignorance of foolish men:

1 Peter 2:13-15

When Your Child Becomes Rebellious Toward God

Wait on the LORD: be of good courage, and he shall strengthen thine heart: wait, I say, on the LORD.

Psalms 27:14

Our soul waiteth for the LORD: he is our help and our shield.

Psalms 33:20

Delight thyself also in the LORD; and he shall give thee the desires of thine heart.

Commit thy way unto the LORD; trust also in him; and he shall bring it to pass.

Psalms 37:4,5

Cast thy burden upon the LORD, and he shall sustain thee: he shall never suffer the righteous to be moved.

Psalms 55:22

For the LORD will not cast off his people, neither will he forsake his inheritance.

Psalms 94:14

I wait for the LORD, my soul doth wait, and in his word do I hope.

Psalms 130:5

The LORD will perfect that which concerneth me: thy mercy, O LORD, endureth for ever: forsake not the works of thine own hands.

Psalms 138:8

Children's children are the crown of old men; and the glory of children are their fathers.

Proverbs 17:6

Correct thy son, and he shall give thee rest; yea, he shall give delight unto thy soul.

Proverbs 29:17

Fear thou not; for I am with thee: be not dismayed; for I am thy God: I will strengthen thee; yea, I will help thee; yea, I will uphold thee with the right hand of my righteousness.

Isaiah 41:10

And all thy children shall be taught of the LORD; and great shall be the peace of thy children.

Isaiah 54:13

And he shall turn the heart of the fathers to the children, and the heart of the children to their fathers, lest I come and smite the earth with a curse.

Malachi 4:6

For we walk by faith, not by sight:

2 Corinthians 5:7

And, ye fathers, provoke not your children to wrath: but bring them up in the nurture and admonition of the Lord.

Ephesians 6:4

Let us hold fast the profession of our faith without wavering; for he is faithful that promised;

Hebrews 10:23

Now faith is the substance of things hoped for, the evidence of things not seen.

But without faith it is impossible to please him: for he that cometh to God must believe that he is, and that he is a rewarder of them that diligently seek him.

Hebrews 11:1,6

That the trial of your faith, being much more precious than of gold that perisheth, though it be tried with fire, might be found unto praise and honour and glory at the appearing of Jesus Christ:

1 Peter 1:7

But ye are a chosen generation, a royal priesthood, an holy nation, a peculiar people; that ye should shew forth the praises of him who hath called you out of darkness into his marvellous light:

1 Peter 2:9

Casting all your care upon him; for he careth for you.

1 Peter 5:7

When Your Child Becomes Lazy and Disinterested

Moreover as for me, God forbid that I should sin against the LORD in ceasing to pray for you: but I will teach you the good and the right way:

1 Samuel 12:23

And there were four leprous men at the entering in of the gate: and they said one to another, Why sit we here until we die? If we say, We will enter into the city, then the famine is in the city, and we shall die there: and if we sit still here, we die also. Now therefore come, and let us fall unto the host of the Syrians: if they save us alive, we shall live; and if they kill us, we shall but die.

2 Kings 7:3,4

I will instruct thee and teach thee in the way which thou shalt go: I will guide thee with mine eye.

Psalms 32:8

Why art thou cast down, O my soul? and why art thou disquieted within me? hope in God: for I shall yet praise him, who is the health of my countenance, and my God.

Psalms 43:5

Happy is he that hath the God of Jacob for his help, whose hope is in the LORD his God:

Psalms 146:5

A wise man will hear, and will increase learning; and a man of understanding shall attain unto wise counsels:

Proverbs 1:5

Hope deferred maketh the heart sick: but when the desire cometh, it is a tree of life.

Proverbs 13:12

The soul of the sluggard desireth, and hath nothing: but the soul of the diligent shall be made fat.

Proverbs 13:4

Whatsoever thy hand findeth to do, do it with thy might; for there is no work, nor device, nor knowledge, nor wisdom, in the grave, whither thou goest.

Ecclesiastes 9:10

By much slothfulness the building decayeth; and through idleness of the hands the house droppeth through.

Ecclesiastes 10:18

Then the king, when he heard these words, was sore displeased with himself, and set his heart on Daniel to deliver him: and he laboured till the going down of the sun to deliver him.

Daniel 6:14

Let your light so shine before men, that they may see your good works, and glorify your Father which is in heaven.

Matthew 5:16

Now the God of hope fill you with all joy and peace in believing, that ye may abound in hope, through the power of the Holy Ghost.

Romans 15:13

Put on the whole armour of God, that ye may be able to stand against the wiles of the devil.

Wherefore take unto you the whole armour of God, that ye may be able to withstand in the evil day, and having done all, to stand.

Praying always with all prayer and supplication in the Spirit, and watching thereunto with all perseverance and supplication for all saints;

Ephesians 6:11,13,18

And the peace of God, which passeth all understanding, shall keep your hearts and minds through Christ Jesus.

Philippians 4:7

And whatsoever ye do, do it heartily, as to the Lord, and not unto men;

Colossians 3:23

Walk in wisdom toward them that are without, redeeming the time.

Colossians 4:5

When Your Child Begins To Withdraw From You

I sought the LORD, and he heard me, and delivered me from all my fears.

Psalms 34:4

Be still, and know that I am God:

Psalms 46:10

He will not suffer thy foot to be moved: he that keepeth thee will not slumber.

Psalms 121:3

For I was an hungred, and ye gave me meat: I was thirsty, and ye gave me drink: I was a stranger, and ye took me in:

Naked, and ye clothed me: I was sick, and ye visited me: I was in prison, and ye came unto me.

Then shall the righteous answer him, saying, Lord, when saw we thee an hungred, and fed thee? or thirsty, and gave thee drink?

When saw we thee a stranger, and took thee in? or naked, and clothed thee?

Or when saw we thee sick, or in prison, and came unto thee?

And the King shall answer and say unto them, Verily I say unto you, Inasmuch as ye have done it unto one of the least of these my brethren, ye have done it unto me.

Matthew 25:35-40

In your patience possess ye your souls.

Luke 21:19

I will not leave you comfortless: I will come to you.

John 14:18

And not only so, but we glory in tribulations also: knowing that tribulation worketh patience;

And patience, experience; and experience, hope:

And hope maketh not ashamed; because the love of God is shed abroad in our hearts by the Holy Ghost which is given unto us.

Romans 5:3-5

Bear ye one another's burdens, and so fulfil the law of Christ.

Galatians 6:2

For God is not unrighteous to forget your work and labour of love, which ye have shewed toward his name, in that ye have ministered to the saints, and do minister.

Hebrews 6:10

If ye fulfil the royal law according to the scripture, Thou shalt love thy neighbour as thyself, ye do well:

James 2:8

But whoso hath this world's good, and seeth his brother have need, and shutteth up his bowels of compassion from him, how dwelleth the love of God in him?

My little children, let us not love in word, neither in tongue; but in deed and in truth.

1 John 3:17,18

When Your Child Encounters Peer Pressure

The LORD also will be a refuge for the oppressed, a refuge in times of trouble.

Psalms 9:9

I will love thee, O LORD, my strength.

The LORD is my rock, and my fortress, and my deliverer; my God, my strength, in whom I will trust; my buckler, and the horn of my salvation, and my high tower.

Psalms 18:1,2

My flesh and my heart faileth: but God is the strength of my heart, and my portion for ever.

Psalms 73:26

A thousand shall fall at thy side, and ten thousand at thy right hand; but it shall not come nigh thee.

There shall no evil befall thee, neither shall any plague come nigh thy dwelling.

Psalms 91:7,10

Bless the LORD, O my soul, and forget not all his benefits:

Who satisfieth thy mouth with good things; so that thy youth is renewed like the eagle's.

Psalms 103:2,5

He sent his word, and healed them, and delivered them from their destructions.

Psalms 107:20

Peace be within thy walls, and prosperity within thy palaces.

Psalms 122:7

It is vain for you to rise up early, to sit up late, to eat the bread of sorrows: for so he giveth his beloved sleep.

Psalms 127:2

When thou liest down, thou shalt not be afraid: yea, thou shalt lie down, and thy sleep shall be sweet.

Proverbs 3:24

The wicked are overthrown, and are not: but the house of the righteous shall stand.

Proverbs 12:7

But they that wait upon the LORD shall renew their strength; they shall mount up with wings as eagles; they shall run, and not be weary; and they shall walk, and not faint.

Isaiah 40:31

Surely he hath borne our griefs, and carried our sorrows: yet we did esteem him stricken, smitten of God, and afflicted.

Isaiah 53:4

Verily I say unto you, Whatsoever ye shall bind on earth shall be bound in heaven: and whatsoever ye shall loose on earth shall be loosed in heaven.

Matthew 18:18

Let not your heart be troubled: ye believe in God, believe also in me.

Peace I leave with you, my peace I give unto you: not as the world giveth, give I unto you. Let not your heart be troubled, neither let it be afraid.

John 14:1, 27

Be careful for nothing; but in every thing by prayer and supplication with thanksgiving let your requests be made known unto God.

And the peace of God, which passeth all understanding, shall keep your hearts and minds through Christ Jesus.

Philippians 4:6, 7

Casting all your care upon him; for he careth for you.

1 Peter 5:7

When Your Child Is Jealous of Your Attention Shown to Others

I will bless the LORD, who hath given me counsel: my reins also instruct me in the night seasons.

I have set the LORD always before me: because he is at my right hand, I shall not be moved.

Therefore my heart is glad, and my glory rejoiceth: my flesh also shall rest in hope.

Psalms 16:7-9

Behold, thou desirest truth in the inward parts: and in the hidden part thou shalt make me to know wisdom.

Create in me a clean heart, O God; and renew a right spirit within me.

Psalms 51:6,10

In God I will praise his word, in God I have put my trust; I will not fear what flesh can do unto me.

Psalms 56:4

Teach me thy way, O LORD; I will walk in thy truth: unite my heart to fear thy name.

Psalms 86:11

Trust in the LORD with all thine heart; and lean not unto thine own understanding.

In all thy ways acknowledge him, and he shall direct thy paths.

For the LORD shall be thy confidence,

Proverbs 3:5,6,26a

The fear of man bringeth a snare: but whoso putteth his trust in the LORD shall be safe.

Proverbs 29:25

Behold, God is my salvation; I will trust, and not be afraid: for the LORD JEHOVAH is my strength and my song; he also is become my salvation.

Isaiah 12:2

Charity suffereth long, and is kind; charity envieth not; charity vaunteth not itself, is not puffed up,

Doth not behave itself unseemly, seeketh not her own, is not easily provoked, thinketh no evil;

1 Corinthians 13:4,5

For the weapons of our warfare are not carnal, but mighty through God to the pulling down of strong holds;

2 Corinthians 10:4

Finally, my brethren, be strong in the Lord, and in the power of his might.

Ephesians 6:10

Finally, brethren, whatsoever things are true, whatsoever things are honest, whatsoever things are just, whatsoever things are pure, whatsoever things are lovely, whatsoever things are of good report; if there be any virtue, and if there be any praise, think on these things.

Philippians 4:8

If any of you lack wisdom, let him ask of God, that giveth to all men liberally, and upbraideth not; and it shall be given him.

James 1:5

Beloved, think it not strange concerning the fiery trial which is to try you, as though some strange thing happened unto you:

1 Peter 4:12

When Your Child Acquires a Poor Self-Image

And God said, Let us make man in our image, after our likeness: and let them have dominion over the fish of the sea, and over the fowl of the air, and over the cattle, and over all the earth, and over every creeping thing that creepeth upon the earth.

So God created man in his own image, in the image of God created he him; male and female created he them. Genesis 1:26,27

Of the Rock that begat thee thou art unmindful, and hast forgotten God that formed thee.

Deuteronomy 32:18

David said moreover, The LORD that delivered me out of the paw of the lion, and out of the paw of the bear, he will deliver me out of the hand of this Philistine. And Saul said unto David, Go, and the LORD be with thee.

1 Samuel 17:37

But thou, O LORD, art a shield for me; my glory, and the lifter up of mine head.

Psalms 3:3

I will not be afraid of ten thousands of people, that have set themselves against me round about.

Psalms 3:6

The LORD is my light and my salvation; whom shall I fear? the LORD is the strength of my life; of whom shall I be afraid?

Though an host should encamp against me, my heart shall not fear: though war should rise against me, in this will I be confident.

For in the time of trouble he shall hide me in his pavilion: in the secret of his tabernacle shall he hide me; he shall set me up upon a rock.

Psalms 27:1,3,5

It is better to trust in the LORD than to put confidence in man.

Psalms 118:8

Thy word have I hid in mine heart, that I might not sin against thee.

Psalms 119:11

For the LORD shall be thy confidence, and shall keep thy foot from being taken.

Proverbs 3:26

In the fear of the LORD is strong confidence: and his children shall have a place of refuge.

Proverbs 14:26

But now thus saith the LORD that created thee, O Jacob, and he that formed thee, O Israel, Fear not: for I have redeemed thee, I have called thee by thy name; thou art mine.

Even every one that is called by my name: for I have created him for my glory, I have formed him; yea, I have made him.

This people have I formed for myself; they shall shew forth my praise.

Isaiah 43:1,7,21

Thus saith the LORD, thy redeemer, and he that formed thee from the womb, I am the LORD that maketh all things; that stretcheth forth the heavens alone; that spreadeth abroad the earth by myself;

Isaiah 44:24

Before I formed thee in the belly I knew thee; and before thou camest forth out of the womb I sanctified thee, and I ordained thee a prophet unto the nations.

Jeremiah 1:5

Ye have not chosen me, but I have chosen you, and ordained you, that ye should go and bring forth fruit, and that your fruit should remain: that whatsoever ye shall ask of the Father in my name, he may give it you.

John 15:16

And changed the glory of the uncorruptible God into an image made like to corruptible man, and to birds, and four-footed beasts, and creeping things.

Romans 1:23

For who hath known the mind of the Lord, that he may instruct him? But we have the mind of Christ.

1 Corinthians 2:16

In whom the god of this world hath blinded the minds of them which believe not, lest the light of the glorious gospel of Christ, who is the image of God, should shine unto them.

2 Corinthians 4:4

Being confident of this very thing, that he which hath begun a good work in you will perform it until the day of Jesus Christ:

Philippians 1:6

Let nothing be done through strife or vainglory; but in lowliness of mind let each esteem other better than themselves.

Look not every man on his own things, but every man also on the things of others.

Let this mind be in you, which was also in Christ Jesus:

Philippians 2:3-5

Who is the image of the invisible God, the firstborn of every creature:

Colossians 1:15

And have put on the new man, which is renewed in knowledge after the image of him that created him:

Colossians 3:10

Ye are of God, little children, and have overcome them: because greater is he that is in you, than he that is in the world.

They are of the world: therefore speak they of the world, and the world heareth them.

We are of God: he that knoweth God heareth us; he that is not of God heareth not us. Hereby know we the spirit of truth, and the spirit of error.

1 John 4:4-6

When Your Child Becomes Unforgiving Toward You

Commit thy way unto the LORD; trust also in him; and he shall bring it to pass.

Psalms 37:5

Commit thy works unto the LORD, and thy thoughts shall be established.

Proverbs 16:3

Blessed are the peacemakers: for they shall be called the children of God.

Matthew 5:9

And forgive us our debts, as we forgive our debtors.

And lead us not into temptation, but deliver us from evil: For thine is the kingdom, and the power, and the glory, for ever. Amen.

For if ye forgive men their trespasses, your heavenly Father will also forgive you:

But if ye forgive not men their trespasses, neither will your Father forgive your trespasses.

Matthew 6:12-15

Judge not, and ye shall not be judged: condemn not, and ye shall not be condemned: forgive, and ye shall be forgiven:

Luke 6:37

Then said Jesus, Father, forgive them; for they know not what they do. And they parted his raiment, and cast lots.

Luke 23:34

Charity suffereth long, and is kind; charity envieth not; charity vaunteth not itself, is not puffed up,

1 Corinthians 13:4

To whom ye forgive any thing, I forgive also: for if I forgave any thing, to whom I forgave it, for your sakes forgave I it in the person of Christ;

Lest Satan should get an advantage of us: for we are not ignorant of his devices.

2 Corinthians 2:10,11

Casting down imaginations, and every high thing that exalteth itself against the knowledge of God, and bringing into captivity every thought to the obedience of Christ;

2 Corinthians 10:5

Wherefore putting away lying, speak every man truth with his neighbour: for we are members one of another.

Be ye angry, and sin not: let not the sun go down upon your wrath:

Neither give place to the devil.

And be ye kind one to another, tender-hearted, forgiving one another, even as God for Christ's sake hath forgiven you.

Ephesians 4:25-27,32

Finally, brethren, whatsoever things are true, whatsoever things are honest, whatsoever things are just, whatsoever things are pure, whatsoever things are lovely, whatsoever things are of good report; if there be any virtue, and if there be any praise, think on these things.

I know both how to be abased, and I know how to abound: every where and in all things I am instructed both to be full and to be hungry, both to abound and to suffer need.

I can do all things through Christ which strengtheneth me.

But my God shall supply all your need according to his riches in glory by Christ Jesus.

Philippians 4:8,12,13,19

For we know him that hath said, Vengeance belongeth unto me, I will recompense, saith the Lord. And again, The Lord shall judge his people.

Hebrews 10:30

Forbearing one another, and forgiving one another, if any man have a quarrel against any: even as Christ forgave you, so also do ye.

And above all these things put on charity, which is the bond of perfectness.

Colossians 3:13,14

If any of you lack wisdom, let him ask of God, that giveth to all men liberally, and upbraideth not; and it shall be given him.

James 1:5

But if ye have bitter envying and strife in your hearts, glory not, and lie not against the truth.

For where envying and strife is, there is confusion and every evil work.

But the wisdom that is from above is first pure, then peaceable, gentle, and easy to be intreated, full of mercy and good fruits, without partiality, and without hypocrisy.

And the fruit of righteousness is sown in peace of them that make peace.

James 3:14,16-18

Confess your faults one to another, and pray one for another, that ye may be healed. The effectual fervent prayer of a righteous man availeth much.

James 5:16

When Your Child Becomes Quarrelsome

And Samuel said, Hath the LORD as great delight in burnt offerings and sacrifices, as in obeying the voice of the LORD? Behold, to obey is better than sacrifice, and to hearken than the fat of rams.

For rebellion is as the sin of witchcraft, and stubbornness is as iniquity and idolatry. Because thou hast rejected the word of the LORD, he hath also rejected thee from being king.

1 Samuel 15:22,23

The discretion of a man deferreth his anger; and it is his glory to pass over a transgression.

Proverbs 19:11

It is an honour for a man to cease from strife: but every fool will be meddling.

Proverbs 20:3

If the spirit of the ruler rise up against thee, leave not thy place; for yielding pacifieth great offences.

Ecclesiastes 10:4

If ye be willing and obedient, ye shall eat the good of the land: But if ye refuse and rebel, ye shall be devoured with the sword: for the mouth of the LORD hath spoken it.
Isaiah 1:19,20

Blessed are the peacemakers: for they shall be called the children of God.
Matthew 5:9

If it be possible, as much as lieth in you, live peaceably with all men.
Romans 12:18

Charity suffereth long, and is kind; charity envieth not;charity vaunteth not itself, is not puffed up,

Doth not behave itself unseemly, seeketh not her own, is not easily provoked, thinketh no evil;

Rejoiceth not in iniquity, but rejoiceth in the truth;

Beareth all things, believeth all things, hopeth all things,endureth all things.
1 Corinthians 13:4-7

Now we exhort you, brethren, warn them that are unruly,
1 Thessalonians 5:14a

And the servant of the Lord must not strive; but be gentle unto all men, apt to teach, patient,

2 Timothy 2:24

To speak evil of no man, to be no brawlers, but gentle, shewing all meekness unto all men.

Titus 3:2

Follow peace with all men, and holiness, without which no man shall see the Lord:

Hebrews 12:14

And the fruit of righteousness is sown in peace of them that make peace.

James 3:18

Likewise, ye younger, submit yourselves unto the elder. Yea, all of you be subject one to another, and be clothed with humility: for God resisteth the proud, and giveth grace to the humble.

Humble yourselves therefore under the mighty hand of God, that he may exalt you in due time:

1 Peter 5:5,6

When Your Child Must Cope With Parental Disharmony

For thou art my rock and my fortress; therefore for thy name's sake lead me, and guide me.

Pull me out of the net that they have laid privily for me: for thou art my strength.

Into thine hand I commit my spirit: thou hast redeemed me, O LORD God of truth.

Psalms 31:3-5

Thou art my hiding place; thou shalt preserve me from trouble; thou shalt compass me about with songs of deliverance.

Psalms 32:7

Commit thy way unto the LORD; trust also in him; and he shall bring it to pass.

And he shall bring forth thy righteousness as the light, and thy judgment as the noonday.

Rest in the LORD, and wait patiently for him: fret not thyself because of him who prospereth in his way, because of the man who bringeth wicked devices to pass.

Psalms 37:5-7

For in thee, O LORD, do I hope: thou wilt hear, O Lord my God.

Psalms 38:15

In my distress I cried unto the LORD, and he heard me.

Deliver my soul, O LORD, from lying lips, and from a deceitful tongue.

Psalms 120:1-2

Though I walk in the midst of trouble, thou wilt revive me: thou shalt stretch forth thine hand against the wrath of mine enemies, and thy right hand shall save me.

Psalms 138:7

These six things doth the LORD hate: yea, seven are an abomination unto him:

A proud look, a lying tongue, and hands that shed innocent blood,

An heart that deviseth wicked imaginations, feet that be swift in running to mischief,

A false witness that speaketh lies, and he that soweth discord among brethren.

Proverbs 6:16-19

Commit thy works unto the LORD, and thy thoughts shall be established.

Proverbs 16:3

Say not, I will do so to him as he hath done to me: I will render to the man according to his work.

Proverbs 24:29

When thou passest through the waters, I will be with thee; and through the rivers, they shall not overflow thee: when thou walkest through the fire, thou shalt not be burned; neither shall the flame kindle upon thee.

Isaiah 43:2

And the LORD shall guide thee continually, and satisfy thy soul in drought, and make fat thy bones: and thou shalt be like a watered garden, and like a spring of water, whose waters fail not.

Isaiah 58:11

I the LORD search the heart, I try the reins, even to give every man according to his ways, and according to the fruit of his doings.

Jeremiah 17:10

The LORD is good, a strong hold in the day of trouble; and he knoweth them that trust in him.

Nahum 1:7

And when ye stand praying, forgive, if ye have ought against any: that your Father also which is in heaven may forgive you your trespasses.

But if ye do not forgive, neither will your Father which is in heaven forgive your trespasses.

Mark 11:25,26

And who is he that will harm you, if ye be followers of that which is good?

1 Peter 3:13

Casting all your care upon him; for he careth for you.

1 Peter 5:7

When Your Child Becomes Sick

And the LORD will take away from thee all sickness, and will put none of the evil diseases of Egypt, which thou knowest, upon thee; but will lay them upon all them that hate thee.

Deuteronomy 7:15

Bless the LORD, O my soul, and forget not all his benefits:

Who forgiveth all thine iniquities; who healeth all thy diseases;

Psalms 103:2,3

My son, attend to my words; incline thine ear unto my sayings.

Let them not depart from thine eyes; keep them in the midst of thine heart.

For they are life unto those that find them, and health to all their flesh.

Proverbs 4:20-22

Surely he hath borne our griefs, and carried our sorrows: yet we did esteem him stricken, smitten of God, and afflicted.

But he was wounded for our transgressions, he was bruised for our iniquities: the chastisement of our peace was upon him; and with his stripes we are healed.

Isaiah 53:4,5

Heal me, O LORD, and I shall be healed; save me, and I shall be saved: for thou art my praise.

Jeremiah 17:14

For I will restore health unto thee, and I will heal thee of thy wounds, saith the LORD;

Jeremiah 30:17a

And Jesus saith unto him, I will come and heal him.

Matthew 8:7

Jesus Christ the same yesterday, and to day, and for ever.

Hebrews 13:8

Is any among you afflicted? let him pray. Is any merry? let him sing psalms.

Is any sick among you? let him call for the elders of the church; and let them pray over him, anointing him with oil in the name of the Lord:

And the prayer of faith shall save the sick, and the Lord shall raise him up; and if he have committed sins, they shall be forgiven him.

Confess your faults one to another, and pray one for another, that ye may be healed. The effectual fervent prayer of a righteous man availeth much.

James 5:13-16

Beloved, I wish above all things that thou mayest prosper and be in health, even as thy soul prospereth.

3 John 1:2

When Your Child Has Thoughts of Suicide

So God created man in his own image, in the image of God created he him; male and female created he them.

Genesis 1:27

Of the Rock that begat thee thou art unmindful, and hast forgotten God that formed thee.

Deuteronomy 32:18

One man of you shall chase a thousand: for the LORD your God, he it is that fighteth for you, as he hath promised you.

Joshua 23:10

He will keep the feet of his saints, and the wicked shall be silent in darkness; for by strength shall no man prevail.

1 Samuel 2:9

David said moreover, The LORD that delivered me out of the paw of the lion, and out of the paw of the bear, he will deliver me out of the hand of this Philistine. And Saul said unto David, Go, and the LORD be with thee.

1 Samuel 17:37

But thou, O LORD, art a shield for me; my glory, and the lifter up of mine head.

Psalms 3:3

I will not be afraid of ten thousands of people, that have set themselves against me round about.

Psalms 3:6

The LORD is my light and my salvation; whom shall I fear? the LORD is the strength of my life; of whom shall I be afraid?

Though an host should encamp against me, my heart shall not fear: though war should rise against me, in this will I be confident.

For in the time of trouble he shall hide me in his pavilion: in the secret of his tabernacle shall he hide me; he shall set me up upon a rock.

Psalms 27:1,3,5

It is better to trust in the LORD than to put confidence in man.

Psalms 118:8

Thy word have I hid in mine heart, that I might not sin against thee.

Psalms 119:11

For the LORD shall be thy confidence, and shall keep thy foot from being taken.

Proverbs 3:26

In the fear of the LORD is strong confidence: and his children shall have a place of refuge.

Proverbs 14:26

But now thus saith the LORD that created thee, O Jacob, and he that formed thee, O Israel, Fear not: for I have redeemed thee, I have called thee by thy name; thou art mine.

Even every one that is called by my name: for I have created him for my glory, I have formed him; yea, I have made him.

This people have I formed for myself;
they shall shew forth my praise.

Isaiah 43:1, 7, 21

Thus saith the LORD, thy redeemer,
and he that formed thee from the womb, I
am the LORD that maketh all things; that
stretcheth forth the heavens alone; that
spreadeth abroad the earth by myself;

Isaiah 44:24

Before I formed thee in the belly I
knew thee; and before thou camest forth
out of the womb I sanctified thee, and I
ordained thee a prophet unto the nations.

Jeremiah 1:5

For who hath known the mind of the
Lord, that he may instruct him? But we have
the mind of Christ.

1 Corinthians 2:16

In whom the god of this world hath
blinded the minds of them which believe
not, lest the light of the glorious gospel of
Christ, who is the image of God, should
shine unto them.

2 Corinthians 4:4

Being confident of this very thing, that he which hath begun a good work in you will perform it until the day of Jesus Christ:

Philippians 1:6

Look not every man on his own things, but every man also on the things of others.

Let this mind be in you, which was also in Christ Jesus:

Philippians 2:4,5

And have put on the new man, which is renewed in knowledge after the image of him that created him:

Colossians 3:10

Ye are of God, little children, and have overcome them: because greater is he that is in you, than he that is in the world.

They are of the world: therefore speak they of the world, and the world heareth them.

We are of God: he that knoweth God heareth us; he that is not of God heareth not us. Hereby know we the spirit of truth, and the spirit of error.

1 John 4:4-6

When Your Child Does Not Want To Attend Church

Only take heed to thyself, and keep thy soul diligently, lest thou forget the things which thine eyes have seen, and lest they depart from thy heart all the days of thy life: but teach them thy sons, and thy sons' sons;

Deuteronomy 4:9

And these words, which I command thee this day, shall be in thine heart:

And thou shalt teach them diligently unto thy children, and shalt talk of them when thou sittest in thine house, and when thou walkest by the way, and when thou liest down, and when thou risest up.

Deuteronomy 6:6,7

And ye shall teach them your children, speaking of them when thou sittest in thine house, and when thou walkest by the way, when thou liest down, and when thou risest up.

Deuteronomy 11:19

For he established a testimony in Jacob, and appointed a law in Israel, which he commanded our fathers, that they should make them known to their children:

That the generation to come might know them, even the children which should be born; who should arise and declare them to their children:

That they might set their hope in God, and not forget the works of God, but keep his commandments:

Psalms 78:5-7

A good man leaveth an inheritance to his children's children: and the wealth of the sinner is laid up for the just.

Proverbs 13:22

The just man walketh in his integrity: his children are blessed after him.

Proverbs 20:7

Train up a child in the way he should go: and when he is old, he will not depart from it.

Proverbs 22:6

Through wisdom is an house builded; and by understanding it is established:

Proverbs 24:3

Correct thy son, and he shall give thee rest; yea, he shall give delight unto thy soul.

Proverbs 29:17

Tell ye your children of it, and let your children tell their children, and their children another generation.

Joel 1:3

But seek ye first the kingdom of God, and his righteousness; and all these things shall be added unto you.

Matthew 6:33

And, ye fathers, provoke not your children to wrath: but bring them up in the nurture and admonition of the Lord.

Ephesians 6:4

But if any provide not for his own, and specially for those of his own house, he hath denied the faith, and is worse than an infidel.

1 Timothy 5:8

When Your Child Is Heartbroken by Divorce

For the LORD thy God is a merciful God; he will not forsake thee, neither destroy thee, nor forget the covenant of thy fathers which he sware unto them.

Deuteronomy 4:31

Be strong and of a good courage, fear not, nor be afraid of them: for the LORD thy God, he it is that doth go with thee; he will not fail thee, nor forsake thee.

Deuteronomy 31:6

For the LORD will not forsake his people for his great name's sake: because it hath pleased the LORD to make you his people.

1 Samuel 12:22

And they that know thy name will put their trust in thee: for thou, LORD, hast not forsaken them that seek thee.

Psalms 9:10

When my father and my mother forsake me, then the LORD will take me up.

Teach me thy way, O LORD, and lead me in a plain path, because of mine enemies.

Psalms 27:10,11

I have been young, and now am old; yet have I not seen the righteous forsaken, nor his seed begging bread.

Psalms 37:25

Why art thou cast down, O my soul? and why art thou disquieted within me? hope in God: for I shall yet praise him, who is the health of my countenance, and my God.

Psalms 43:5

Because he hath set his love upon me, therefore will I deliver him: I will set him on high, because he hath known my name.

He shall call upon me, and I will answer him: I will be with him in trouble; I will deliver him, and honour him.

Psalms 91:14,15

For the LORD will not cast off his people, neither will he forsake his inheritance.

Psalms 94:14

When the poor and needy seek water, and there is none, and their tongue faileth for thirst, I the LORD will hear them, I the God of Israel will not forsake them.

Isaiah 41:17

Can a woman forget her sucking child, that she should not have compassion on the son of her womb? yea, they may forget, yet will I not forget thee.

Behold, I have graven thee upon the palms of my hands; thy walls are continually before me.

Isaiah 49:15,16

Thou shalt no more be termed Forsaken; neither shall thy land any more be termed Desolate: but thou shalt be called Hephzibah, and thy land Beulah: for the LORD delighteth in thee, and thy land shall be married.

Isaiah 62:4

The Spirit of the Lord is upon me, because he hath anointed me to preach the gospel to the poor; he hath sent me to heal the brokenhearted, to preach deliverance to the captives, and recovering of sight to the blind, to set at liberty them that are bruised,

To preach the acceptable year of the Lord.

Luke 4:18,19

Persecuted, but not forsaken; cast down, but not destroyed;

2 Corinthians 4:9

Casting all your care upon him; for he careth for you.

1 Peter 5:7

When Your Child Is Beyond Your Daily Influence

The LORD lift up his countenance upon thee, and give thee peace.

Numbers 6:26

For the LORD thy God is a merciful God; he will not forsake thee, neither destroy thee, nor forget the covenant of thy fathers which he sware unto them.

Deuteronomy 4:31

Be strong and of a good courage, fear not, nor be afraid of them: for the LORD thy God, he it is that doth go with thee; he will not fail thee, nor forsake thee.

And the LORD, he it is that doth go before thee; he will be with thee, he will not fail thee, neither forsake thee: fear not, neither be dismayed.

Deuteronomy 31:6,8

Wait on the LORD: be of good courage, and he shall strengthen thine heart: wait, I say, on the LORD.

Psalms 27:14

Delight thyself also in the LORD; and he shall give thee the desires of thine heart.

I have been young, and now am old; yet have I not seen the righteous forsaken, nor his seed begging bread.

Psalms 37:4,25

Lo, children are an heritage of the LORD: and the fruit of the womb is his reward.

As arrows are in the hand of a mighty man; so are children of the youth.

Happy is the man that hath his quiver full of them: they shall not be ashamed,

Psalms 127:3-5a

A man's heart deviseth his way: but the LORD directeth his steps.

Proverbs 16:9

Train up a child in the way he should go: and when he is old, he will not depart from it.

Proverbs 22:6

The father of the righteous shall greatly rejoice: and he that begetteth a wise child shall have joy of him.

Proverbs 23:24

Correct thy son, and he shall give thee rest; yea, he shall give delight unto thy soul.

Proverbs 29:17

Can a woman forget her sucking child, that she should not have compassion on the son of her womb? yea, they may forget, yet will I not forget thee.

Behold, I have graven thee upon the palms of my hands; thy walls are continually before me.

Isaiah 49:15,16

Teaching them to observe all things whatsoever I have commanded you: and, lo, I am with you alway, even unto the end of the world. Amen.

Matthew 28:20

That the trial of your faith, being much more precious than of gold that perisheth, though it be tried with fire, might be found unto praise and honour and glory at the appearing of Jesus Christ:

1 Peter 1:7

Casting all your care upon him; for he careth for you.

1 Peter 5:7

When You Have Made Mistakes in Raising Your Child

That then the LORD thy God will turn thy captivity, and have compassion upon thee, and will return and gather thee from all the nations, whither the LORD thy God hath scattered thee.

Deuteronomy 30:3

If my people, which are called by my name, shall humble themselves, and pray, and seek my face, and turn from their wicked ways; then will I hear from heaven, and will forgive their sin, and will heal their land.

2 Chronicles 7:14

That which I see not teach thou me: if I have done iniquity, I will do no more.

Job 34:32

He restoreth my soul: he leadeth me in the paths of righteousness for his name's sake.

Psalms 23:3

Wait on the LORD: be of good courage, and he shall strengthen thine heart: wait, I say, on the LORD.

Psalms 27:14

Our soul waiteth for the LORD: he is our help and our shield.

Psalms 33:20

Create in me a clean heart, O God; and renew a right spirit within me.

Cast me not away from thy presence; and take not thy holy spirit from me.

Restore unto me the joy of thy salvation; and uphold me with thy free spirit.

Psalms 51:10-12

Cast thy burden upon the LORD, and he shall sustain thee: he shall never suffer the righteous to be moved.

Psalms 55:22

I wait for the LORD, my soul doth wait, and in his word do I hope.

Psalms 130:5

The LORD will perfect that which concerneth me: thy mercy, O LORD, endureth for ever: forsake not the works of thine own hands.

Psalms 138:8

Fear thou not; for I am with thee: be not dismayed; for I am thy God: I will strengthen thee; yea, I will help thee; yea, I will uphold thee with the right hand of my righteousness.

Isaiah 41:10

For I will pour water upon him that is thirsty, and floods upon the dry ground: I will pour my spirit upon thy seed, and my blessing upon thine offspring:

Isaiah 44:3

And I will restore to you the years that the locust hath eaten, the cankerworm, and the caterpillar, and the palmerworm, my great army which I sent among you.

Joel 2:25

And Jesus said unto them, Because of your unbelief: for verily I say unto you, If ye have faith as a grain of mustard seed, ye shall say unto this mountain, Remove hence to yonder place; and it shall remove; and nothing shall be impossible unto you.

Matthew 17:20

And they said, Believe on the Lord Jesus Christ, and thou shalt be saved, and thy house.

Acts 16:31

And Paul, earnestly beholding the council, said, Men and brethren, I have lived in all good conscience before God until this day.

Acts 23:1

And we know that all things work together for good to them that love God, to them who are the called according to his purpose.

Romans 8:28

But ye are a chosen generation, a royal priesthood, an holy nation, a peculiar people; that ye should shew forth the praises of him who hath called you out of darkness into his marvellous light:

1 Peter 2:9

Casting all your care upon him; for he careth for you.

1 Peter 5:7

When Your Child Seems Unappreciative

But the children of Belial said, How shall this man save us? And they despised him, and brought him no presents. But he held his peace.

1 Samuel 10:27

He restoreth my soul: he leadeth me in the paths of righteousness for his name's sake.

Psalms 23:3

Hide me from the secret counsel of the wicked; from the insurrection of the workers of iniquity:

Psalms 64:2

Better is the end of a thing than the beginning thereof: and the patient in spirit is better than the proud in spirit. Be not hasty in thy spirit to be angry: for anger resteth in the bosom of fools.

Ecclesiastes 7:8,9

Blessed are they which are persecuted for righteousness' sake: for theirs is the kingdom of heaven.

Blessed are ye, when men shall revile you, and persecute you, and shall say all manner of evil against you falsely, for my sake.

Rejoice, and be exceeding glad: for great is your reward in heaven: for so persecuted they the prophets which were before you.

Matthew 5:10-12

Then came Peter to him, and said, Lord, how oft shall my brother sin against me, and I forgive him? till seven times?

Jesus saith unto him, I say not unto thee, Until seven times: but, Until seventy times seven.

Matthew 18:21,22

And when ye stand praying, forgive, if ye have ought against any: that your Father also which is in heaven may forgive you your trespasses.

Mark 11:25

Take heed to yourselves: If thy brother trespass against thee, rebuke him; and if he repent, forgive him.

Luke 17:3

Be not overcome of evil, but overcome evil with good.

Romans 12:21

But he that doeth wrong shall receive for the wrong which he hath done: and there is no respect of persons.

Colossians 3:25

For we know him that hath said, Vengeance belongeth unto me, I will recompense, saith the Lord. And again, The Lord shall judge his people.

Hebrews 10:30

So that we may boldly say, The Lord is my helper, and I will not fear what man shall do unto me.

Hebrews 13:6

Let all bitterness, and wrath, and anger, and clamour, and evil speaking, be put away from you, with all malice:

And be ye kind one to another, tender-hearted, forgiving one another, even as God for Christ's sake hath forgiven you.

Ephesians 4:31,32

For what glory is it, if, when ye be buffeted for your faults, ye shall take it patiently? but if, when ye do well, and suffer for it, ye take it patiently, this is acceptable with God.

1 Peter 2:20

Not rendering evil for evil, or railing for railing: but contrariwise blessing; knowing that ye are thereunto called, that ye should inherit a blessing.

For he that will love life, and see good days, let him refrain his tongue from evil, and his lips that they speak no guile:

1 Peter 3:9,10

Beloved, think it not strange concerning the fiery trial which is to try you, as though some strange thing happened unto you:

But rejoice, inasmuch as ye are partakers of Christ's sufferings; that, when his glory shall be revealed, ye may be glad also with exceeding joy.

If ye be reproached for the name of Christ, happy are ye; for the spirit of glory and of God resteth upon you: on their part he is evil spoken of, but on your part he is glorified.

1 Peter 4:12-14

When Your Child Seems Irresponsible

Be strong and of a good courage, fear not, nor be afraid of them: for the LORD thy God, he it is that doth go with thee; he will not fail thee, nor forsake thee.

Deuteronomy 31:6

Wait on the LORD: be of good courage, and he shall strengthen thine heart: wait, I say, on the LORD.

Psalms 27:14

Thy word have I hid in mine heart, that I might not sin against thee.

Psalms 119:11

When thou goest, it shall lead thee; when thou sleepest, it shall keep thee; and when thou awakest, it shall talk with thee.

For the commandment is a lamp; and the law is light; and reproofs of instruction are the way of life:

Proverbs 6:22,23

He that is slow to wrath is of great understanding: but he that is hasty of spirit exalteth folly.

Proverbs 14:29

A wholesome tongue is a tree of life: but perverseness therein is a breach in the spirit.

Proverbs 15:4

Better it is to be of an humble spirit with the lowly, than to divide the spoil with the proud.

He that handleth a matter wisely shall find good: and whoso trusteth in the LORD, happy is he.

The wise in heart shall be called prudent: and the sweetness of the lips increaseth learning.

Proverbs 16:19-21

The beginning of strife is as when one letteth out water: therefore leave off contention, before it be meddled with.

He that hath knowledge spareth his words: and a man of understanding is of an excellent spirit.

Proverbs 17:14,27

Better is the end of a thing than the beginning thereof: and the patient in spirit is better than the proud in spirit.

Ecclesiastes 7:8

And the spirit of the LORD shall rest upon him, the spirit of wisdom and understanding, the spirit of counsel and might, the spirit of knowledge and of the fear of the LORD;

Isaiah 11:2

And they were not able to resist the wisdom and the spirit by which he spake.

Acts 6:10

Not slothful in business; fervent in spirit; serving the Lord;

If it be possible, as much as lieth in you, live peaceably with all men.

Romans 12:11,18

For God hath not given us the spirit of fear; but of power, and of love, and of a sound mind.

2 Timothy 1:7

If any of you lack wisdom, let him ask of God, that giveth to all men liberally, and upbraideth not; and it shall be given him.

James 1:5

But the wisdom that is from above is first pure, then peaceable, gentle, and easy to be intreated, full of mercy and good fruits, without partiality, and without hypocrisy.

James 3:17

When Your Child Is Not Committed to God

The eternal God is thy refuge, and underneath are the everlasting arms: and he shall thrust out the enemy from before thee; and shall say, Destroy them.

Deuteronomy 33:27

The steps of a good man are ordered by the LORD: and he delighteth in his way.

Psalms 37:23

Be still, and know that I am God: I will be exalted among the heathen, I will be exalted in the earth.

Psalms 46:10

And call upon me in the day of trouble: I will deliver thee, and thou shalt glorify me.

Psalms 50:15

Cast thy burden upon the LORD, and he shall sustain thee: he shall never suffer the righteous to be moved.

Psalms 55:22

My flesh and my heart faileth: but God is the strength of my heart, and my portion for ever.

Psalms 73:26

In the multitude of my thoughts within me thy comforts delight my soul.

Psalms 94:19

He healeth the broken in heart, and bindeth up their wounds.

Psalms 147:3

Fear thou not; for I am with thee: be not dismayed; for I am thy God: I will strengthen thee; yea, I will help thee; yea, I will uphold thee with the right hand of my righteousness.

Behold, all they that were incensed against thee shall be ashamed and confounded: they shall be as nothing; and they that strive with thee shall perish.

Thou shalt seek them, and shalt not find them, even them that contended with thee: they that war against thee shall be as nothing, and as a thing of nought.

For I the LORD thy God will hold thy right hand, saying unto thee, Fear not; I will help thee.

Isaiah 41:10-13

I came not to call the righteous, but sinners to repentance.

Luke 5:32

For the Son of man is come to seek and to save that which was lost.

Luke 19:10

In your patience possess ye your souls.

Luke 21:19

Not that I speak in respect of want: for I have learned, in whatsoever state I am, therewith to be content.

I know both how to be abased, and I know how to abound: every where and in all things I am instructed both to be full and to be hungry, both to abound and to suffer need.

I can do all things through Christ which strengtheneth me.

Philippians 4:11-13

Thou therefore endure hardness, as a good soldier of Jesus Christ.

2 Timothy 2:3

The Lord is not slack concerning his promise, as some men count slackness; but is longsuffering to us-ward, not willing that any should perish, but that all should come to repentance.

2 Peter 3:9

When You Fear the Consequences of His Lifestyle

I had fainted, unless I had believed to see the goodness of the LORD in the land of the living.

Psalms 27:13

Commit thy way unto the LORD; trust also in him; and he shall bring it to pass.

Psalms 37:5

Blessed are they that keep his testimonies, and that seek him with the whole heart.

Give me understanding, and I shall keep thy law; yea, I shall observe it with my whole heart.

Thy word have I hid in mine heart, that I might not sin against thee.

Thy word is a lamp unto my feet, and a light unto my path.

Psalms 119:2,34,11,105

Trust in the LORD with all thine heart; and lean not unto thine own understanding.

Proverbs 3:5

Correct thy son, and he shall give thee rest; yea, he shall give delight unto thy soul.

Proverbs 29:17

For the Lord GOD will help me; therefore shall I not be confounded: therefore have I set my face like a flint, and I know that I shall not be ashamed.

Isaiah 50:7

And ye shall seek me, and find me, when ye shall search for me with all your heart.

Jeremiah 29:13

Behold, I give unto you power to tread on serpents and scorpions, and over all the power of the enemy: and nothing shall by any means hurt you.

Luke 10:19

So likewise, whosoever he be of you that forsaketh not all that he hath, he cannot be my disciple.

Luke 14:33

Peace I leave with you, my peace I give unto you: not as the world giveth, give I unto you. Let not your heart be troubled, neither let it be afraid.

John 14:27

And they said, Believe on the Lord Jesus Christ, and thou shalt be saved, and thy house.

Acts 16:31

Let all bitterness, and wrath, and anger, and clamour, and evil speaking, be put away from you, with all malice:

And be ye kind one to another, tender-hearted, forgiving one another, even as God for Christ's sake hath forgiven you.

Ephesians 4:31,32

And, ye fathers, provoke not your children to wrath: but bring them up in the nurture and admonition of the Lord.

Ephesians 6:4

But what things were gain to me, those I counted loss for Christ.

Philippians 3:7

For God hath not given us the spirit of fear; but of power, and of love, and of a sound mind.

2 Timothy 1:7

There is no fear in love; but perfect love casteth out fear: because fear hath torment. He that feareth is not made perfect in love.

1 John 4:18

When Your Child Blames You for His Problems

I will bless the LORD, who hath given me counsel: my reins also instruct me in the night seasons.

I have set the LORD always before me: because he is at my right hand, I shall not be moved.

Psalms 16:7,8

Many are the afflictions of the righteous: but the LORD delivereth him out of them all.

Psalms 34:19

Cast thy burden upon the LORD, and he shall sustain thee: he shall never suffer the righteous to be moved.

Psalms 55:22

He only is my rock and my salvation; he is my defence; I shall not be greatly moved.

Psalms 62:2

The LORD will perfect that which concerneth me: thy mercy, O LORD, endureth for ever: forsake not the works of thine own hands.

Psalms 138:8

Trust in the LORD with all thine heart; and lean not unto thine own understanding.

In all thy ways acknowledge him, and he shall direct thy paths.

Proverbs 3:5,6

A soft answer turneth away wrath: but grievous words stir up anger.

The tongue of the wise useth knowledge aright: but the mouth of fools poureth out foolishness.

Proverbs 15:1,2

He that handleth a matter wisely shall find good: and whoso trusteth in the LORD, happy is he.

Proverbs 16:20

The fear of man bringeth a snare: but whoso putteth his trust in the LORD shall be safe.

Proverbs 29:25

Behold, God is my salvation; I will trust, and not be afraid: for the LORD JEHOVAH is my strength and my song; he also is become my salvation.

Isaiah 12:2

Thou wilt keep him in perfect peace, whose mind is stayed on thee: because he trusteth in thee.

Trust ye in the LORD for ever: for in the LORD JEHOVAH is everlasting strength:

Isaiah 26:3,4

O LORD, be gracious unto us; we have waited for thee: be thou their arm every morning, our salvation also in the time of trouble.

Isaiah 33:2

Fear thou not; for I am with thee: be not dismayed; for I am thy God: I will strengthen thee; yea, I will help thee; yea, I will uphold thee with the right hand of my righteousness.

Isaiah 41:10

Therefore I will look unto the LORD; I will wait for the God of my salvation: my God will hear me.

Micah 7:7

What shall we then say to these things? If God be for us, who can be against us?

Romans 8:31

Be ye angry, and sin not: let not the sun go down upon your wrath:

Let all bitterness, and wrath, and anger, and clamour, and evil speaking, be put away from you, with all malice:

Ephesians 4:26,31

Looking diligently lest any man fail of the grace of God; lest any root of bitterness springing up trouble you, and thereby many be defiled;

Hebrews 12:15

Beloved, think it not strange concerning the fiery trial which is to try you, as though some strange thing happened unto you:

But rejoice, inasmuch as ye are partakers of Christ's sufferings; that, when his glory shall be revealed, ye may be glad also with exceeding joy.

1 Peter 4:12,13

YOUR WIFE

When Your Wife Seems Unsupportive of Your Dreams and Goals

The LORD is my light and my salvation; whom shall I fear? the LORD is the strength of my life; of whom shall I be afraid?

Though an host should encamp against me, my heart shall not fear: though war should rise against me, in this will I be confident.

Wait on the LORD: be of good courage, and he shall strengthen thine heart: wait, I say, on the LORD.

Psalms 27:1,3,14

For thou art my rock and my fortress; therefore for thy name's sake lead me, and guide me.

Pull me out of the net that they have laid privily for me: for thou art my strength.

Psalms 31:3,4

Thou art my hiding place; thou shalt preserve me from trouble; thou shalt compass me about with songs of deliverance.

I will instruct thee and teach thee in the way which thou shalt go: I will guide thee with mine eye.

Psalms 32:7,8

My soul melteth for heaviness: strengthen thou me according unto thy word.

Psalms 119:28

Hatred stirreth up strifes: but love covereth all sins.

Proverbs 10:12

A friend loveth at all times, and a brother is born for adversity.

Proverbs 17:17

Therefore all things whatsoever ye would that men should do to you, do ye even so to them: for this is the law and the prophets.

Matthew 7:12

A new commandment I give unto you, That ye love one another; as I have loved you, that ye also love one another.

John 13:34

I know both how to be abased, and I know how to abound: every where and in all things I am instructed both to be full and to be hungry, both to abound and to suffer need.

I can do all things through Christ which strengtheneth me.

But my God shall supply all your need according to his riches in glory by Christ Jesus.

Philippians 4:12,13,19

Forbearing one another, and forgiving one another, if any man have a quarrel against any: even as Christ forgave you, so also do ye.

And above all these things put on charity, which is the bond of perfectness.

Colossians 3:13,14

If any of you lack wisdom, let him ask of God, that giveth to all men liberally, and upbraideth not; and it shall be given him.

James 1:5

But if ye have bitter envying and strife in your hearts, glory not, and lie not against the truth.

For where envying and strife is, there is confusion and every evil work.

But the wisdom that is from above is first pure, then peaceable, gentle, and easy to be intreated, full of mercy and good fruits, without partiality, and without hypocrisy.

And the fruit of righteousness is sown in peace of them that make peace.

James 3:14,16-18

Confess your faults one to another, and pray one for another, that ye may be healed. The effectual fervent prayer of a righteous man availeth much.

James 5:16

When Your Wife Disagrees With You About the Children's Discipline

If thou doest well, shalt thou not be accepted? and if thou doest not well, sin lieth at the door. And unto thee shall be his desire, and thou shalt rule over him. Genesis 4:7

And these words, which I command thee this day, shall be in thine heart:

And thou shalt teach them diligently unto thy children, and shalt talk of them when thou sittest in thine house, and when thou walkest by the way, and when thou liest down, and when thou risest up.

And thou shalt bind them for a sign upon thine hand, and they shall be as frontlets between thine eyes.

And thou shalt write them upon the posts of thy house, and on thy gates.

Deuteronomy 6:6-9

This book of the law shall not depart out of thy mouth; but thou shalt meditate therein day and night, that thou mayest observe to do according to all that is written therein: for then thou shalt make thy way prosperous, and then thou shalt have good success.

Joshua 1:8

Lo, children are an heritage of the LORD: and the fruit of the womb is his reward.

Psalms 127:3

Children's children are the crown of old men; and the glory of children are their fathers.

Proverbs 17:6

Train up a child in the way he should go: and when he is old, he will not depart from it.

Proverbs 22:6

And the LORD shall guide thee continually, and satisfy thy soul in drought, and make fat thy bones: and thou shalt be like a watered garden, and like a spring of water, whose waters fail not.

Isaiah 58:11

And he shall turn the heart of the fathers to the children, and the heart of the children to their fathers, lest I come and smite the earth with a curse.

Malachi 4:6

Let all bitterness, and wrath, and anger, and clamour, and evil speaking, be put away from you, with all malice:

And be ye kind one to another, tenderhearted, forgiving one another, even as God for Christ's sake hath forgiven you.

Ephesians 4:31,32

But thou, O man of God, flee these things; and follow after righteousness, godliness, faith, love, patience, meekness.

1 Timothy 6:11

When Your Wife Seems Overly Critical or Abusive

Though an host should encamp against me, my heart shall not fear: though war should rise against me, in this will I be confident.

Wait on the LORD: be of good courage, and he shall strengthen thine heart: wait, I say, on the LORD.

Psalms 27:3,14

For thou art my rock and my fortress; therefore for thy name's sake lead me, and guide me.

Psalms 31:3

Thou art my hiding place; thou shalt preserve me from trouble; thou shalt compass me about with songs of deliverance.

I will instruct thee and teach thee in the way which thou shalt go: I will guide thee with mine eye.

Psalms 32:7,8

A soft answer turneth away wrath: but grievous words stir up anger.

A scorner loveth not one that re-proveth him: neither will he go unto the wise.

Proverbs 15:1,12

Blessed are ye, when men shall revile you, and persecute you, and shall say all manner of evil against you falsely, for my sake.

Rejoice, and be exceeding glad: for great is your reward in heaven: for so persecuted they the prophets which were before you.

Matthew 5:11,12

But I say unto you, Love your enemies, bless them that curse you, do good to them that hate you, and pray for them which despitefully use you, and persecute you;

That ye may be the children of your Father which is in heaven: for he maketh his sun to rise on the evil and on the good, and sendeth rain on the just and on the unjust.

Be ye therefore perfect, even as your Father which is in heaven is perfect.

Matthew 5:44,45,48

But I say unto you, That every idle word that men shall speak, they shall give account thereof in the day of judgment.

For by thy words thou shalt be justified, and by thy words thou shalt be condemned.
Matthew 12:36,37

Moreover if thy brother shall trespass against thee, go and tell him his fault between thee and him alone: if he shall hear thee, thou hast gained thy brother.
Matthew 18:15

Let no corrupt communication proceed out of your mouth, but that which is good to the use of edifying, that it may minister grace unto the hearers.

And grieve not the holy Spirit of God, whereby ye are sealed unto the day of redemption.

Let all bitterness, and wrath, and anger, and clamour, and evil speaking, be put away from you, with all malice:

And be ye kind one to another, tenderhearted, forgiving one another, even as God for Christ's sake hath forgiven you.
Ephesians 4:29-32

For we know him that hath said, Vengeance belongeth unto me, I will recompense, saith the Lord. And again, The Lord shall judge his people.

Hebrews 10:30

Forbearing one another, and forgiving one another, if any man have a quarrel against any: even as Christ forgave you, so also do ye.

And above all these things put on charity, which is the bond of perfectness.

Colossians 3:13,14

But if ye have bitter envying and strife in your hearts, glory not, and lie not against the truth.

For where envying and strife is, there is confusion and every evil work.

But the wisdom that is from above is first pure, then peaceable, gentle, and easy to be intreated, full of mercy and good fruits, without partiality, and without hypocrisy.

And the fruit of righteousness is sown in peace of them that make peace.

James 3:14,16-18

Not rendering evil for evil, or railing for railing: but contrariwise blessing; knowing that ye are thereunto called, that ye should inherit a blessing.

For he that will love life, and see good days, let him refrain his tongue from evil, and his lips that they speak no guile:

For the eyes of the Lord are over the righteous, and his ears are open unto their prayers: but the face of the Lord is against them that do evil.

Having a good conscience; that, whereas they speak evil of you, as of evildoers, they may be ashamed that falsely accuse your good conversation in Christ.

For it is better, if the will of God be so, that ye suffer for well doing, than for evil doing.

1 Peter 3:9,10,12,16,17

When Your Wife Seems Jealous or Overprotective

Keep thy tongue from evil, and thy lips from speaking guile.

Psalms 34:13

Fret not thyself because of evildoers, neither be thou envious against the workers of iniquity.

Psalms 37:1

Envy thou not the oppressor, and choose none of his ways.

Proverbs 3:31

A sound heart is the life of the flesh: but envy the rottenness of the bones.

Proverbs 14:30

Death and life are in the power of the tongue: and they that love it shall eat the fruit thereof.

Proverbs 18:21

Be not thou envious against evil men, neither desire to be with them.

Proverbs 24:1

Set me as a seal upon thine heart, as a seal upon thine arm: for love is strong as death; jealousy is cruel as the grave: the coals thereof are coals of fire, which hath a most vehement flame.

Song of Solomon 8:6

Judge not, that ye be not judged.

Matthew 7:1

Let us walk honestly, as in the day; not in rioting and drunkenness, not in chambering and wantonness, not in strife and envying.

Romans 13:13

For ye are yet carnal: for whereas there is among you envying, and strife, and divisions, are ye not carnal, and walk as men?

1 Corinthians 3:3

And they that are Christ's have crucified the flesh with the affections and lusts.

If we live in the Spirit, let us also walk in the Spirit.

Let us not be desirous of vain glory, provoking one another, envying one another.

Galatians 5:24-26

Let no corrupt communication proceed out of your mouth, but that which is good to the use of edifying, that it may minister grace unto the hearers.

Let all bitterness, and wrath, and anger, and clamour, and evil speaking, be put away from you, with all malice:

Ephesians 4:29,31

Wherefore laying aside all malice, and all guile, and hypocrisies, and envies, and all evil speakings,

As newborn babes, desire the sincere milk of the word, that ye may grow thereby:

1 Peter 2:1,2

Not rendering evil for evil, or railing for railing: but contrariwise blessing; knowing that ye are thereunto called, that ye should inherit a blessing.

For he that will love life, and see good days, let him refrain his tongue from evil, and his lips that they speak no guile:

1 Peter 3:9,10

But ye, beloved, building up yourselves on your most holy faith, praying in the Holy Ghost,

Jude 1:20

When Your Wife Has Responsibilities Away From Home

I will bless the LORD, who hath given me counsel: my reins also instruct me in the night seasons.

Psalms 16:7

As for God, his way is perfect: the word of the LORD is tried: he is a buckler to all those that trust in him.

Psalms 18:30

Teach me thy way, O LORD, and lead me in a plain path, because of mine enemies.

Psalms 27:11

Great peace have they which love thy law: and nothing shall offend them.

Psalms 119:165

The LORD will perfect that which concerneth me: thy mercy, O LORD, endureth for ever: forsake not the works of thine own hands.

Psalms 138:8

Trust in the LORD with all thine heart; and lean not unto thine own understanding.

In all thy ways acknowledge him, and he shall direct thy paths.

Proverbs 3:5,6

Counsel is mine, and sound wisdom: I am understanding; I have strength.

Proverbs 8:14

Understanding is a wellspring of life unto him that hath it: but the instruction of fools is folly.

The heart of the wise teacheth his mouth, and addeth learning to his lips.

Proverbs 16:22, 23

Through wisdom is an house builded; and by understanding it is established:

And by knowledge shall the chambers be filled with all precious and pleasant riches.

Proverbs 24:3, 4

Behold, God is my salvation; I will trust, and not be afraid: for the LORD JEHOVAH is my strength and my song; he also is become my salvation.

Isaiah 12:2

For my thoughts are not your thoughts, neither are your ways my ways, saith the LORD.

For as the heavens are higher than the earth, so are my ways higher than your ways, and my thoughts than your thoughts.

Isaiah 55:8, 9

Call unto me, and I will answer thee, and shew thee great and mighty things, which thou knowest not.

Jeremiah 33:3

Can two walk together, except they be agreed?

Amos 3:3

And I say unto you, Ask, and it shall be given you; seek, and ye shall find; knock, and it shall be opened unto you.

Luke 11:9

Then opened he their understanding, that they might understand the scriptures,

Luke 24:45

Forbearing one another, and forgiving one another, if any man have a quarrel against any: even as Christ forgave you, so also do ye.

Colossians 3:13

YOUR WORK

When You Have Become a Workaholic

Blessed is the man that walketh not in the counsel of the ungodly, nor standeth in the way of sinners, nor sitteth in the seat of the scornful.

But his delight is in the law of the LORD; and in his law doth he meditate day and night.

And he shall be like a tree planted by the rivers of water, that bringeth forth his fruit in his season; his leaf also shall not wither; and whatsoever he doeth shall prosper.

Psalms 1:1,2,3

I will bless the LORD, who hath given me counsel: my reins also instruct me in the night seasons.

Psalms 16:7

Shew me thy ways, O LORD; teach me thy paths.

Psalms 25:4

One thing have I desired of the LORD, that will I seek after; that I may dwell in the house of the LORD all the days of my life, to behold the beauty of the LORD, and to inquire in his temple.

For in the time of trouble he shall hide me in his pavilion: in the secret of his tabernacle shall he hide me; he shall set me up upon a rock.

Psalms 27:4,5

I will instruct thee and teach thee in the way which thou shalt go: I will guide thee with mine eye.

Psalms 32:8

God is our refuge and strength, a very present help in trouble.

Psalms 46:1

Behold, thou desirest truth in the inward parts: and in the hidden part thou shalt make me to know wisdom.

Psalms 51:6

I will say of the LORD, He is my refuge and my fortress: my God; in him will I trust.

Psalms 91:2

Unto the upright there ariseth light in the darkness: he is gracious, and full of compassion, and righteous.

Psalms 112:4

The LORD is on my side; I will not fear: what can man do unto me?

It is better to trust in the LORD than to put confidence in man.

Psalms 118:6,8

For the LORD giveth wisdom: out of his mouth cometh knowledge and understanding.

Proverbs 2:6

Trust in the LORD with all thine heart; and lean not unto thine own understanding.

In all thy ways acknowledge him, and he shall direct thy paths.

Proverbs 3:5,6

Without counsel purposes are disappointed: but in the multitude of counsellors they are established.

Proverbs 15:22

And thine ears shall hear a word behind thee, saying, This is the way, walk ye in it, when ye turn to the right hand, and when ye turn to the left.

Isaiah 30:21

And I will bring the blind by a way that they knew not; I will lead them in paths that they have not known: I will make darkness light before them, and crooked things straight. These things will I do unto them, and not forsake them.

Isaiah 42:16

Thus saith the LORD, thy Redeemer, the Holy One of Israel; I am the LORD thy God which teacheth thee to profit, which leadeth thee by the way that thou shouldest go.

Isaiah 48:17

Howbeit when he, the Spirit of truth, is come, he will guide you into all truth: for he shall not speak of himself; but whatsoever he shall hear, that shall he speak: and he will shew you things to come.

He shall glorify me: for he shall receive of mine, and shall shew it unto you.

John 16:13,14

What shall we then say to these things? If God be for us, who can be against us?

Romans 8:31

If any of you lack wisdom, let him ask of God, that giveth to all men liberally, and upbraideth not; and it shall be given him.

James 1:5

When You Feel Unusual Stress

The LORD also will be a refuge for the oppressed, a refuge in times of trouble.

Psalms 9:9

I will love thee, O LORD, my strength.

The LORD is my rock, and my fortress, and my deliverer; my God, my strength, in whom I will trust; my buckler, and the horn of my salvation, and my high tower.

Psalms 18:1,2

My flesh and my heart faileth: but God is the strength of my heart, and my portion for ever.

Psalms 73:26

Yea, the LORD shall give that which is good; and our land shall yield her increase.

Psalms 85:12

A thousand shall fall at thy side, and ten thousand at thy right hand; but it shall not come nigh thee.

There shall no evil befall thee, neither shall any plague come nigh thy dwelling.

Psalms 91:7,10

Bless the LORD, O my soul, and forget not all his benefits:

Who satisfieth thy mouth with good things; so that thy youth is renewed like the eagle's.

Psalms 103:2,5

He sent his word, and healed them, and delivered them from their destructions.

Psalms 107:20

Peace be within thy walls, and prosperity within thy palaces.

Psalms 122:7

It is vain for you to rise up early, to sit up late, to eat the bread of sorrows: for so he giveth his beloved sleep.

Psalms 127:2

When thou liest down, thou shalt not be afraid: yea, thou shalt lie down, and thy sleep shall be sweet.

Proverbs 3:24

The wicked are overthrown, and are not: but the house of the righteous shall stand.

Proverbs 12:7

Verily I say unto you, Whatsoever ye shall bind on earth shall be bound in heaven: and whatsoever ye shall loose on earth shall be loosed in heaven.

Matthew 18:18

Let not your heart be troubled: ye believe in God, believe also in me.

Peace I leave with you, my peace I give unto you: not as the world giveth, give I unto you. Let not your heart be troubled, neither let it be afraid.

John 14:1,27

Be careful for nothing; but in every thing by prayer and supplication with thanksgiving let your requests be made known unto God.

And the peace of God, which passeth all understanding, shall keep your hearts and minds through Christ Jesus.

Philippians 4:6,7

Casting all your care upon him; for he careth for you.

1 Peter 5:7

When Your Efforts Seem Unappreciated by Others

Be strong and of a good courage, fear not, nor be afraid of them: for the LORD thy God, he it is that doth go with thee; he will not fail thee, nor forsake thee.

Deuteronomy 31:6

And they that know thy name will put their trust in thee: for thou, LORD, hast not forsaken them that seek thee.

Psalms 9:10

As for God, his way is perfect: the word of the LORD is tried: he is a buckler to all those that trust in him.

Psalms 18:30

The LORD hear thee in the day of trouble; the name of the God of Jacob defend thee;

Send thee help from the sanctuary, and strengthen thee out of Zion;

Psalms 20:1,2

Many are the afflictions of the righteous: but the LORD delivereth him out of them all.

Psalms 34:19

Why art thou cast down, O my soul? and why art thou disquieted within me? hope in God: for I shall yet praise him, who is the health of my countenance, and my God.

Psalms 43:5

My soul, wait thou only upon God; for my expectation is from him.

Psalms 62:5

Because he hath set his love upon me, therefore will I deliver him: I will set him on high, because he hath known my name.

He shall call upon me, and I will answer him: I will be with him in trouble; I will deliver him, and honour him.

Psalms 91:14,15

I wait for the LORD, my soul doth wait, and in his word do I hope.

Psalms 130:5

So shalt thou find favour and good understanding in the sight of God and man.

Trust in the LORD with all thine heart; and lean not unto thine own understanding.

In all thy ways acknowledge him, and he shall direct thy paths.

Proverbs 3:4-6

Keep thy heart with all diligence; for out of it are the issues of life.

Proverbs 4:23

Fear thou not; for I am with thee: be not dismayed; for I am thy God: I will strengthen thee; yea, I will help thee; yea, I will uphold thee with the right hand of my righteousness.

Isaiah 41:10

Behold, I have graven thee upon the palms of my hands; thy walls are continually before me.

Isaiah 49:16

Ask, and it shall be given you; seek, and ye shall find; knock, and it shall be opened unto you:

For every one that asketh receiveth; and he that seeketh findeth; and to him that knocketh it shall be opened.

Matthew 7:7,8

Lo, I am with you alway, even unto the end of the world. Amen.

Matthew 28:20b

Behold, I give unto you power to tread on serpents and scorpions, and over all the power of the enemy: and nothing shall by any means hurt you.

Luke 10:19

And we know that all things work together for good to them that love God, to them who are the called according to his purpose.

For I am persuaded, that neither death, nor life, nor angels, nor principalities, nor powers, nor things present, nor things to come,

Nor height, nor depth, nor any other creature, shall be able to separate us from the love of God, which is in Christ Jesus our Lord.

Romans 8:28,38,39

What shall we then say to these things? If God be for us, who can be against us?

Romans 8:31

So that we may boldly say, The Lord is my helper, and I will not fear what man shall do unto me.

Hebrews 13:6

Casting all your care upon him; for he careth for you.

1 Peter 5:7

When You Feel Like a Failure

But he knoweth the way that I take: when he hath tried me, I shall come forth as gold.

Job 23:10

He will keep the feet of his saints, and the wicked shall be silent in darkness; for by strength shall no man prevail.

1 Samuel 2:9

I will both lay me down in peace, and sleep: for thou, LORD, only makest me dwell in safety.

Psalms 4:8

He that dwelleth in the secret place of the most High shall abide under the shadow of the Almighty.

I will say of the LORD, He is my refuge and my fortress: my God; in him will I trust.

Psalms 91:1,2

As far as the east is from the west, so far hath he removed our transgressions from us.

Psalms 103:12

When thou liest down, thou shalt not be afraid: yea, thou shalt lie down, and thy sleep shall be sweet.

Proverbs 3:24

Thou wilt keep him in perfect peace, whose mind is stayed on thee: because he trusteth in thee.

Isaiah 26:3

I, even I, am he that blotteth out thy transgressions for mine own sake, and will not remember thy sins.

Isaiah 43:25

Let the wicked forsake his way, and the unrighteous man his thoughts: and let him return unto the LORD, and he will have mercy upon him; and to our God, for he will abundantly pardon.

Isaiah 55:7

The LORD thy God in the midst of thee is mighty; he will save, he will rejoice over thee with joy; he will rest in his love, he will joy over thee with singing.

Zephaniah 3:17

For he hath made him to be sin for us, who knew no sin; that we might be made the righteousness of God in him.

2 Corinthians 5:21

But the Lord is faithful, who shall stablish you, and keep you from evil.

2 Thessalonians 3:3

And let the peace of God rule in your hearts, to the which also ye are called in one body; and be ye thankful.

Colossians 3:15

For I will be merciful to their unrighteousness, and their sins and their iniquities will I remember no more.

Hebrews 8:12

Casting all your care upon him; for he careth for you.

1 Peter 5:7

If we confess our sins, he is faithful and just to forgive us our sins, and to cleanse us from all unrighteousness.

1 John 1:9

And they overcame him by the blood of the Lamb, and by the word of their testimony; and they loved not their lives unto the death.

Revelation 12:11

When Others Have Unrealistic Expectations of You

My times are in thy hand: deliver me from the hand of mine enemies, and from them that persecute me.

Psalms 31:15

When a man's ways please the LORD, he maketh even his enemies to be at peace with him.

Proverbs 16:7

Let your light so shine before men, that they may see your good works, and glorify your Father which is in heaven.

But I say unto you, Love your enemies, bless them that curse you, do good to them that hate you, and pray for them which despitefully use you, and persecute you;

Matthew 5:16,44

For verily I say unto you, That whosoever shall say unto this mountain, Be thou removed, and be thou cast into the sea; and shall not doubt in his heart, but shall believe that those things which he saith shall come to pass; he shall have whatsoever he saith.

Mark 11:23

Take heed to yourselves: If thy brother trespass against thee, rebuke him; and if he repent, forgive him.

Luke 17:3

Be not overcome of evil, but overcome evil with good.

Romans 12:21

Let all bitterness, and wrath, and anger, and clamour, and evil speaking, be put away from you, with all malice:

And be ye kind one to another, tenderhearted, forgiving one another, even as God for Christ's sake hath forgiven you.

Ephesians 4:31,32

Let us therefore come boldly unto the throne of grace, that we may obtain mercy, and find grace to help in time of need.

Hebrews 4:16

For God is not unrighteous to forget your work and labour of love, which ye have shewed toward his name, in that ye have ministered to the saints, and do minister.

Hebrews 6:10

For we know him that hath said, Vengeance belongeth unto me, I will recompense, saith the Lord. And again, The Lord shall judge his people.

Hebrews 10:30

When Your Job Is Unfulfilling

Be of good courage, and he shall strengthen your heart, all ye that hope in the LORD.

Psalms 31:24

I will instruct thee and teach thee in the way which thou shalt go: I will guide thee with mine eye.

Psalms 32:8

For in thee, O LORD, do I hope: thou wilt hear, O Lord my God.

Psalms 38:15

Why art thou cast down, O my soul? and why art thou disquieted within me? hope in God: for I shall yet praise him, who is the health of my countenance, and my God.

Psalms 43:5

But I will hope continually, and will yet praise thee more and more.

Psalms 71:14

Happy is he that hath the God of Jacob for his help, whose hope is in the LORD his God:

Psalms 146:5

Keep thy heart with all diligence; for out of it are the issues of life.

Proverbs 4:23

The hand of the diligent shall bear rule: but the slothful shall be under tribute.

Proverbs 12:24

Hope deferred maketh the heart sick: but when the desire cometh, it is a tree of life.

Proverbs 13:12

Love not sleep, lest thou come to poverty; open thine eyes, and thou shalt be satisfied with bread.

Proverbs 20:13

Let not thine heart envy sinners: but be thou in the fear of the LORD all the day long.

For surely there is an end; and thine expectation shall not be cut off.

Proverbs 23:17,18

Whatsoever thy hand findeth to do, do it with thy might;

Ecclesiastes 9:10A

I must work the works of him that sent me, while it is day: the night cometh, when no man can work.

John 9:4

Now the God of hope fill you with all joy and peace in believing, that ye may abound in hope, through the power of the Holy Ghost.

Romans 15:13

Therefore, my beloved brethren, be ye stedfast, unmoveable, always abounding in the work of the Lord, forasmuch as ye know that your labour is not in vain in the Lord.

1 Corinthians 15:58

And God is able to make all grace abound toward you; that ye, always having all sufficiency in all things, may abound to every good work:

2 Corinthians 9:8

For when I am weak, then am I strong.

2 Corinthians 12:10b

That he would grant you, according to the riches of his glory, to be strengthened with might by his Spirit in the inner man;

Ephesians 3:16

And the peace of God, which passeth all understanding, shall keep your hearts and minds through Christ Jesus.

Philippians 4:7

Now faith is the substance of things hoped for, the evidence of things not seen.

But without faith it is impossible to please him: for he that cometh to God must believe that he is, and that he is a rewarder of them that diligently seek him.

Hebrews 11:1,6

And that ye study to be quiet, and to do your own business, and to work with your own hands, as we commanded you;

That ye may walk honestly toward them that are without, and that ye may have lack of nothing.

1 Thessalonians 4:11,12

Wherefore gird up the loins of your mind, be sober, and hope to the end for the grace that is to be brought unto you at the revelation of Jesus Christ;

But the word of the Lord endureth for ever. And this is the word which by the gospel is preached unto you.

1 Peter 1:13,25

When You Make a Major Career Decision

And the LORD, he it is that doth go before thee; he will be with thee, he will not fail thee, neither forsake thee: fear not, neither be dismayed.

Deuteronomy 31:8

Have not I commanded thee? Be strong and of a good courage; be not afraid, neither be thou dismayed: for the LORD thy God is with thee whithersoever thou goest.

Joshua 1:9

Be ye strong therefore, and let not your hands be weak: for your work shall be rewarded.

2 Chronicles 15:7

I will bless the LORD, who hath given me counsel: my reins also instruct me in the night seasons.

Psalms 16:7

Shew me thy ways, O LORD; teach me thy paths.

Psalms 25:4

I will instruct thee and teach thee in the way which thou shalt go: I will guide thee with mine eye.

Psalms 32:8

Many are the afflictions of the righteous: but the LORD delivereth him out of them all.

Psalms 34:19

God is our refuge and strength, a very present help in trouble.

Psalms 46:1

Behold, thou desirest truth in the inward parts: and in the hidden part thou shalt make me to know wisdom.

Psalms 51:6

I will say of the LORD, He is my refuge and my fortress: my God; in him will I trust.

Psalms 91:2

The LORD is on my side; I will not fear: what can man do unto me?

It is better to trust in the LORD than to put confidence in man.

Psalms 118:6,8

For ever, O LORD, thy word is settled in heaven.

Psalms 119:89

For the LORD giveth wisdom: out of his mouth cometh knowledge and understanding.

Proverbs 2:6

Trust in the LORD with all thine heart; and lean not unto thine own understanding.

In all thy ways acknowledge him, and he shall direct thy paths.

Proverbs 3:5,6

My son, attend to my words; incline thine ear unto my sayings. Let them not depart from thine eyes; keep them in the midst of thine heart.

For they are life unto those that find them, and health to all their flesh.

Proverbs 4:20-22

Where no counsel is, the people fall: but in the multitude of counsellors there is safety.

Proverbs 11:14

Without counsel purposes are disappointed: but in the multitude of counsellors they are established.

Proverbs 15:22

The name of the LORD is a strong tower: the righteous runneth into it, and is safe.

Proverbs 18:10

And thine ears shall hear a word behind thee, saying, This is the way, walk ye in it, when ye turn to the right hand, and when ye turn to the left.

Isaiah 30:21

Fear thou not; for I am with thee: be not dismayed; for I am thy God: I will strengthen thee; yea, I will help thee; yea, I will uphold thee with the right hand of my righteousness.

Isaiah 41:10

And I will bring the blind by a way that they knew not; I will lead them in paths that they have not known: I will make darkness light before them, and crooked things straight. These things will I do unto them, and not forsake them.

Isaiah 42:16

Thus saith the LORD, thy Redeemer, the Holy One of Israel; I am the LORD thy God which teacheth thee to profit, which leadeth thee by the way that thou shouldest go.

Isaiah 48:17

Howbeit when he, the Spirit of truth, is come, he will guide you into all truth: for he shall not speak of himself; but whatsoever he shall hear, that shall he speak: and he will shew you things to come.

He shall glorify me: for he shall receive of mine, and shall shew it unto you.

John 16:13,14

What shall we then say to these things? If God be for us, who can be against us?

Romans 8:31

Being confident of this very thing, that he which hath begun a good work in you will perform it until the day of Jesus Christ:

And this I pray, that your love may abound yet more and more in knowledge and in all judgment;

That ye may approve things that are excellent; that ye may be sincere and without offence till the day of Christ;

Philippians 1:6,9,10

If any of you lack wisdom, let him ask of God, that giveth to all men liberally, and upbraideth not; and it shall be given him.

James 1:5

When You Get Fired From Your Job

O LORD my God, in thee do I put my trust: save me from all them that persecute me, and deliver me:

Psalms 7:1

And they that know thy name will put their trust in thee: for thou, LORD, hast not forsaken them that seek thee.

Psalms 9:10

Unto thee, O LORD, do I lift up my soul.

O my God, I trust in thee: let me not be ashamed, let not mine enemies triumph over me.

Psalms 25:1,2

Trust in the LORD, and do good; so shalt thou dwell in the land, and verily thou shalt be fed.

Delight thyself also in the LORD; and he shall give thee the desires of thine heart.

Commit thy way unto the LORD; trust also in him; and he shall bring it to pass.

And he shall bring forth thy righteousness as the light, and thy judgment as the noonday.

For evildoers shall be cut off: but those that wait upon the LORD, they shall inherit the earth.

The steps of a good man are ordered by the LORD: and he delighteth in his way.

I have been young, and now am old; yet have I not seen the righteous forsaken, nor his seed begging bread.

For the LORD loveth judgment, and forsaketh not his saints; they are preserved for ever: but the seed of the wicked shall be cut off.

Psalms 37: 3-6,9,23,25,28

Why art thou cast down, O my soul? and why art thou disquieted in me? hope thou in God: for I shall yet praise him for the help of his countenance.

Psalms 42:5

And call upon me in the day of trouble: I will deliver thee, and thou shalt glorify me.

Psalms 50:15

Because he hath set his love upon me, therefore will I deliver him: I will set him on high, because he hath known my name.

He shall call upon me, and I will answer him: I will be with him in trouble; I will deliver him, and honour him.

Psalms 91:14,15

For the LORD will not cast off his people, neither will he forsake his inheritance.

Psalms 94:14

Though I walk in the midst of trouble, thou wilt revive me: thou shalt stretch forth thine hand against the wrath of mine enemies, and thy right hand shall save me.

The LORD will perfect that which concerneth me: thy mercy, O LORD, endureth for ever: forsake not the works of thine own hands.

Psalms 138:7,8

Say not thou, I will recompense evil; but wait on the LORD, and he shall save thee.

Proverbs 20:22

For if ye forgive men their trespasses, your heavenly Father will also forgive you:

Matthew 6:14

And if he trespass against thee seven times in a day, and seven times in a day turn again to thee, saying, I repent; thou shalt forgive him.

Luke 17:4

Recompense to no man evil for evil. Provide things honest in the sight of all men.

Romans 12:17

Charity suffereth long, and is kind; charity envieth not; charity vaunteth not itself, is not puffed up,

1 Corinthians 13:4

For we wrestle not against flesh and blood, but against principalities, against powers, against the rulers of the darkness of this world, against spiritual wickedness in high places.

Wherefore take unto you the whole armour of God, that ye may be able to withstand in the evil day, and having done all, to stand.

Stand therefore, having your loins girt about with truth, and having on the breastplate of righteousness;

And your feet shod with the preparation of the gospel of peace;

Above all, taking the shield of faith, wherewith ye shall be able to quench all the fiery darts of the wicked.

Ephesians 6:12-16

And the servant of the Lord must not strive; but be gentle unto all men, apt to teach, patient,

2 Timothy 2:24

Notwithstanding the Lord stood with me, and strengthened me; that by me the preaching might be fully known, and that all the Gentiles might hear: and I was delivered out of the mouth of the lion.

And the Lord shall deliver me from every evil work, and will preserve me unto his heavenly kingdom: to whom be glory for ever and ever. Amen.

2 Timothy 4:17,18

Let us therefore come boldly unto the throne of grace, that we may obtain mercy, and find grace to help in time of need.

Hebrews 4:16

Beloved, think it not strange concerning the fiery trial which is to try you, as though some strange thing happened unto you:

But rejoice, inasmuch as ye are partakers of Christ's sufferings; that, when his glory shall be revealed, ye may be glad also with exceeding joy.

1 Peter 4:12,13

YOUR DAILY SCHEDULE

When You Have Over-Booked Your Schedule

The LORD also will be a refuge for the oppressed, a refuge in times of trouble.

Psalms 9:9

Bless the LORD, O my soul, and forget not all his benefits:

Who satisfieth thy mouth with good things; so that thy youth is renewed like the eagle's.

Psalms 103:2,5

Great peace have they which love thy law: and nothing shall offend them.

Psalms 119:165

Quicken me, O LORD, for thy name's sake: for thy righteousness' sake bring my soul out of trouble.

Psalms 143:11

When thou liest down, thou shalt not be afraid: yea, thou shalt lie down, and thy sleep shall be sweet.

Proverbs 3:24

Give instruction to a wise man, and he will be yet wiser: teach a just man, and he will increase in learning.

Proverbs 9:9

The wicked are overthrown, and are not: but the house of the righteous shall stand.

Proverbs 12:7

Open rebuke is better than secret love.

Proverbs 27:5

But they that wait upon the LORD shall renew their strength; they shall mount up with wings as eagles; they shall run, and not be weary; and they shall walk, and not faint.

Isaiah 40:31

For the Lord GOD will help me; therefore shall I not be confounded:

Isaiah 50:7a

There hath no temptation taken you but such as is common to man: but God is faithful, who will not suffer you to be tempted above that ye are able; but will with the temptation also make a way to escape, that ye may be able to bear it.

1 Corinthians 10:13

That he would grant you, according to the riches of his glory, to be strengthened with might by his Spirit in the inner man;

Ephesians 3:16

Finally, my brethren, be strong in the Lord, and in the power of his might.

Ephesians 6:10

Be careful for nothing; but in every thing by prayer and supplication with thanksgiving let your requests be made known unto God.

And the peace of God, which passeth all understanding, shall keep your hearts and minds through Christ Jesus.

I can do all things through Christ which strengtheneth me.

Philippians 4:6,7,13

If any of you lack wisdom, let him ask of God, that giveth to all men liberally, and upbraideth not; and it shall be given him.

James 1:5

When You Feel Disorganized

The LORD is my shepherd; I shall not want.

Psalms 23:1

Shew me thy ways, O LORD; teach me thy paths.

Psalms 25:4

I will instruct thee and teach thee in the way which thou shalt go: I will guide thee with mine eye.

Psalms 32:8

Cast thy burden upon the LORD, and he shall sustain thee: he shall never suffer the righteous to be moved.

Psalms 55:22

Trust in the LORD with all thine heart; and lean not unto thine own understanding.

In all thy ways acknowledge him, and he shall direct thy paths.

For the LORD shall be thy confidence, and shall keep thy foot from being taken.

Proverbs 3:5,6,26

O LORD, I know that the way of man is not in himself: it is not in man that walketh to direct his steps.

Jeremiah 10:23

And he said unto them, "Come ye yourselves apart into a desert place, and rest a while:" for there were many coming and going, and they had no leisure so much as to eat.

Mark 6:31

For God is not the author of confusion, but of peace, as in all churches of the saints.

1 Corinthians 14:33

Therefore, my beloved brethren, be ye stedfast, unmoveable, always abounding in the work of the Lord, forasmuch as ye know that your labour is not in vain in the Lord.

1 Corinthians 15:58

And let us not be weary in well doing: for in due season we shall reap, if we faint not.

Galatians 6:9

Be careful for nothing; but in every thing by prayer and supplication with thanksgiving let your requests be made known unto God.

And the peace of God, which passeth all understanding, shall keep your hearts and minds through Christ Jesus.

Philippians 4:6, 7

For God hath not given us the spirit of fear; but of power, and of love, and of a sound mind.

2 Timothy 1:7

If any of you lack wisdom, let him ask of God, that giveth to all men liberally, and upbraideth not; and it shall be given him.

James 1:5

When You Become Frustrated by Unnecessary Interruptions

Trust in the LORD with all thine heart; and lean not unto thine own understanding.

Proverbs 3:5

Commit thy works unto the LORD, and thy thoughts shall be established.

Proverbs 16:3

The fear of man bringeth a snare: but whoso putteth his trust in the LORD shall be safe.

Proverbs 29:25

Blessed is the man that trusteth in the LORD, and whose hope the LORD is.

For he shall be as a tree planted by the waters, and that spreadeth out her roots by the river, and shall not see when heat cometh, but her leaf shall be green; and shall not be careful in the year of drought, neither shall cease from yielding fruit.

Jeremiah 17:7,8

Take my yoke upon you, and learn of me; for I am meek and lowly in heart: and ye shall find rest unto your souls.

Matthew 11:29

Jesus said unto him, If thou canst believe, all things are possible to him that believeth.

Mark 9:23

And I say unto you, Ask, and it shall be given you; seek, and ye shall find; knock, and it shall be opened unto you.

Luke 11:9

If then God so clothe the grass, which is to day in the field, and to morrow is cast into the oven; how much more will he clothe you, O ye of little faith?

Luke 12:28

Let us therefore come boldly unto the throne of grace, that we may obtain mercy, and find grace to help in time of need.

Hebrews 4:16

That ye be not slothful, but followers of them who through faith and patience inherit the promises.

Hebrews 6:12

Cast not away therefore your confidence, which hath great recompence of reward.

Now the just shall live by faith: but if any man draw back, my soul shall have no pleasure in him.

Hebrews 10:35,38

Let your conversation be without covetousness; and be content with such things as ye have: for he hath said, I will never leave thee, nor forsake thee.

Hebrews 13:5

Casting all your care upon him; for he careth for you.

1 Peter 5:7

When Work Robs You of Important Family Time

Through wisdom is an house builded; and by understanding it is established:

Proverbs 24:3

But seek ye first the kingdom of God, and his righteousness; and all these things shall be added unto you.

Matthew 6:33

And they said, Believe on the Lord Jesus Christ, and thou shalt be saved, and thy house.

Acts 16:31

Rejoicing in hope; patient in tribulation; continuing instant in prayer;

Romans 12:12

Now the God of hope fill you with all joy and peace in believing, that ye may abound in hope, through the power of the Holy Ghost.

Romans 15:13

Charity suffereth long, and is kind; charity envieth not; charity vaunteth not itself, is not puffed up,

Doth not behave itself unseemly, seeketh not her own, is not easily provoked, thinketh no evil;

Rejoiceth not in iniquity, but rejoiceth in the truth;

Beareth all things, believeth all things, hopeth all things, endureth all things.

1 Corinthians 13:4-7

And, ye fathers, provoke not your children to wrath: but bring them up in the nurture and admonition of the Lord.

Ephesians 6:4

One that ruleth well his own house, having his children in subjection with all gravity;

For if a man know not how to rule his own house, how shall he take care of the church of God?

1 Timothy 3:4,5

If any of you lack wisdom, let him ask of God, that giveth to all men liberally, and upbraideth not; and it shall be given him.

James 1:5

When You Need Time Away From the Demands of Others

In my distress I called upon the LORD, and cried to my God: and he did hear my voice out of his temple, and my cry did enter into his ears.

2 Samuel 22:7

God is our refuge and strength, a very present help in trouble. Therefore will not we fear, though the earth be removed, and though the mountains be carried into the midst of the sea;

Psalms 46:1,2

The LORD will perfect that which concerneth me: thy mercy, O LORD, endureth for ever: forsake not the works of thine own hands.

Psalms 138:8

He giveth power to the faint; and to them that have no might he increaseth strength.

Isaiah 40:29

Then said Jesus to them again, Peace be unto you: as my Father hath sent me, even so send I you.

John 20:21

While we look not at the things which are seen, but at the things which are not seen: for the things which are seen are temporal; but the things which are not seen are eternal.

2 Corinthians 4:18

Stand fast therefore in the liberty wherewith Christ hath made us free, and be not entangled again with the yoke of bondage.

This I say then, Walk in the Spirit, and ye shall not fulfil the lust of the flesh.

Galatians 5:1,16

And that ye study to be quiet, and to do your own business, and to work with your own hands, as we commanded you;

That ye may walk honestly toward them that are without, and that ye may have lack of nothing.

1 Thessalonians 4:11,12

Thou therefore endure hardness, as a good soldier of Jesus Christ.

2 Timothy 2:3

Follow peace with all men, and holiness, without which no man shall see the Lord:

Hebrews 12:14

Blessed is the man that endureth temptation: for when he is tried, he shall receive the crown of life, which the Lord hath promised to them that love him.

James 1:12

When Daily Family Devotions Seem Difficult

A good man leaveth an inheritance to his children's children: and the wealth of the sinner is laid up for the just.

Proverbs 13:22

The just man walketh in his integrity: his children are blessed after him.

Proverbs 20:7

Train up a child in the way he should go: and when he is old, he will not depart from it.

Proverbs 22:6

The father of the righteous shall greatly rejoice: and he that begetteth a wise child shall have joy of him.

Proverbs 23:24

Through wisdom is an house builded; and by understanding it is established:

Proverbs 24:3

Correct thy son, and he shall give thee rest; yea, he shall give delight unto thy soul.

Proverbs 29:17

And all thy children shall be taught of the LORD; and great shall be the peace of thy children.

In righteousness shalt thou be established: thou shalt be far from oppression; for thou shalt not fear: and from terror; for it shall not come near thee.

Isaiah 54:13,14

Tell ye your children of it, and let your children tell their children, and their children another generation.

Joel 1:3

But seek ye first the kingdom of God, and his righteousness; and all these things shall be added unto you.

Matthew 6:33

And, ye fathers, provoke not your children to wrath: but bring them up in the nurture and admonition of the Lord.

Ephesians 6:4

Fathers, provoke not your children to anger, lest they be discouraged.

Colossians 3:21

One that ruleth well his own house, having his children in subjection with all gravity;

For if a man know not how to rule his own house, how shall he take care of the church of God?

1 Timothy 3:4,5

But if any provide not for his own, and specially for those of his own house, he hath denied the faith, and is worse than an infidel.

1 Timothy 5:8

YOUR FINANCES

When Your Job Security Is Threatened

The LORD is good, a strong hold in the day of trouble; and he knoweth them that trust in him.

Nahum 1:7

The LORD is my shepherd; I shall not want.

Psalms 23:1

I have been young, and now am old; yet have I not seen the righteous forsaken, nor his seed begging bread.

Psalms 37:25

Honour the LORD with thy substance, and with the firstfruits of all thine increase:

So shall thy barns be filled with plenty, and thy presses shall burst out with new wine.

Proverbs 3:9,10

Seest thou a man diligent in his business? he shall stand before kings; he shall not stand before mean men.

Proverbs 22:29

Whatsoever thy hand findeth to do, do it with thy might;

Ecclesiastes 9:10a

Therefore, my beloved brethren, be ye stedfast, unmoveable, always abounding in the work of the Lord, forasmuch as ye know that your labour is not in vain in the Lord.

1 Corinthians 15:58

But my God shall supply all your need according to his riches in glory by Christ Jesus.

Philippians 4:19

Beloved, I wish above all things that thou mayest prosper and be in health, even as thy soul prospereth.

3 John 1:2

When You Face Bankruptcy

The LORD bless thee, and keep thee:

Numbers 6:24

For the LORD thy God is a merciful God; he will not forsake thee, neither destroy thee, nor forget the covenant of thy fathers which he sware unto them.

Deuteronomy 4:31

Be strong and of a good courage, fear not, nor be afraid of them: for the LORD thy God, he it is that doth go with thee; he will not fail thee, nor forsake thee.

And the LORD, he it is that doth go before thee; he will be with thee, he will not fail thee, neither forsake thee: fear not, neither be dismayed.

Deuteronomy 31:6,8

For there is hope of a tree, if it be cut down, that it will sprout again, and that the tender branch thereof will not cease.

Though the root thereof wax old in the earth, and the stock thereof die in the ground;

Yet through the scent of water it will bud, and bring forth boughs like a plant.

Job 14:7-9

He raiseth up the poor out of the dust, and lifteth up the beggar from the dunghill, to set them among princes, and to make them inherit the throne of glory: for the pillars of the earth are the LORD'S, and he hath set the world upon them.

1 Samuel 2:8

For the needy shall not alway be forgotten: the expectation of the poor shall not perish for ever.

Psalms 9:18

Wait on the LORD: be of good courage, and he shall strengthen thine heart: wait, I say, on the LORD.

Psalms 27:14

My times are in thy hand: deliver me from the hand of mine enemies, and from them that persecute me.

Make thy face to shine upon thy servant: save me for thy mercies' sake.

Psalms 31:15,16

I have been young, and now am old; yet have I not seen the righteous forsaken, nor his seed begging bread.

Psalms 37:25

Vow, and pay unto the LORD your God: let all that be round about him bring presents unto him that ought to be feared.

Psalms 76:11

Honour the LORD with thy substance, and with the firstfruits of all thine increase:

So shall thy barns be filled with plenty, and thy presses shall burst out with new wine.

Proverbs 3:9,10

The LORD will not suffer the soul of the righteous to famish: but he casteth away the substance of the wicked.

He becometh poor that dealeth with a slack hand: but the hand of the diligent maketh rich.

The blessing of the LORD, it maketh rich, and he addeth no sorrow with it.

Proverbs 10:3,4,22

Although the fig tree shall not blossom, neither shall fruit be in the vines; the labour of the olive shall fail, and the fields shall yield no meat; the flock shall be cut off from the fold, and there shall be no herd in the stalls:

Yet I will rejoice in the LORD, I will joy in the God of my salvation.

Habakkuk 3:17,18

Bring ye all the tithes into the storehouse, that there may be meat in mine house, and prove me now herewith, saith the LORD of hosts, if I will not open you the windows of heaven, and pour you out a blessing, that there shall not be room enough to receive it.

And I will rebuke the devourer for your sakes, and he shall not destroy the fruits of your ground; neither shall your vine cast her fruit before the time in the field, saith the LORD of hosts.

And all nations shall call you blessed: for ye shall be a delightsome land, saith the LORD of hosts.

Malachi 3:10-12

And every one that hath forsaken houses, or brethren, or sisters, or father, or mother, or wife, or children, or lands, for my name's sake, shall receive an hundredfold, and shall inherit everlasting life.

Matthew 19:29

Give, and it shall be given unto you; good measure, pressed down, and shaken together, and running over, shall men give into your bosom. For with the same measure that ye mete withal it shall be measured to you again.

Luke 6:38

And he looked up, and saw the rich men casting their gifts into the treasury.

And he saw also a certain poor widow casting in thither two mites.

And he said, Of a truth I say unto you, that this poor widow hath cast in more than they all:

For all these have of their abundance cast in unto the offerings of God: but she of her penury hath cast in all the living that she had.

Luke 21:1-4

Not that I speak in respect of want: for I have learned, in whatsoever state I am, therewith to be content.

I know both how to be abased, and I know how to abound: every where and in all things I am instructed both to be full and to be hungry, both to abound and to suffer need.

I can do all things through Christ which strengtheneth me.

But my God shall supply all your need according to his riches in glory by Christ Jesus.

Philippians 4:11-13,19

Beloved, I wish above all things that thou mayest prosper and be in health, even as thy soul prospereth.

3 John 1:2

When You Need Creative Ideas for Financial Freedom

Now therefore go, and I will be with thy mouth, and teach thee what thou shalt say.

Exodus 4:12

Only be thou strong and very courageous, that thou mayest observe to do according to all the law, which Moses my servant commanded thee: turn not from it to the right hand or to the left, that thou mayest prosper whithersoever thou goest.

Joshua 1:7

But there is a spirit in man: and the inspiration of the Almighty giveth them understanding.

Job 32:8

Then he openeth the ears of men, and sealeth their instruction,

Job 33:16

I will bless the LORD, who hath given me counsel: my reins also instruct me in the night seasons.

Psalms 16:7

I will instruct thee and teach thee in the way which thou shalt go: I will guide thee with mine eye.

Psalms 32:8

For with thee is the fountain of life: in thy light shall we see light.

Psalms 36:9

The LORD will perfect that which concerneth me: thy mercy, O LORD, endureth for ever: forsake not the works of thine own hands.

Psalms 138:8

A wise man will hear, and will increase learning; and a man of understanding shall attain unto wise counsels:

Proverbs 1:5

Wisdom is the principal thing; therefore get wisdom: and with all thy getting get understanding.

Proverbs 4:7

Exalt her, and she shall promote thee: she shall bring thee to honour, when thou dost embrace her.

Proverbs 4:8

I love them that love me; and those that seek me early shall find me.

Proverbs 8:17

Riches and honour are with me; yea, durable riches and righteousness.

Proverbs 8:18

That I may cause those that love me to inherit substance; and I will fill their treasures.

Proverbs 8:21

The thoughts of the righteous are right: but the counsels of the wicked are deceit.

Proverbs 12:5

He that walketh with wise men shall be wise: but a companion of fools shall be destroyed.

Proverbs 13:20

The heart of the prudent getteth knowledge; and the ear of the wise seeketh knowledge.

Proverbs 18:15

So shall the knowledge of wisdom be unto thy soul: when thou hast found it, then there shall be a reward, and thy expectation shall not be cut off.

Proverbs 24:14

Behold, the former things are come to pass, and new things do I declare: before they spring forth I tell you of them.

Isaiah 42:9

Remember ye not the former things, neither consider the things of old.

Behold, I will do a new thing; now it shall spring forth; shall ye not know it? I will even make a way in the wilderness, and rivers in the desert.

Isaiah 43:18,19

For who hath despised the day of small things? for they shall rejoice, and shall see the plummet in the hand of Zerubbabel with those seven; they are the eyes of the LORD, which run to and fro through the whole earth.

Zechariah 4:10

Ask, and it shall be given you; seek, and ye shall find; knock, and it shall be opened unto you:

Matthew 7:7

For which of you, intending to build a tower, sitteth not down first, and counteth the cost, whether he have sufficient to finish it?

Luke 14:28

Knowing that whatsoever good thing any man doeth, the same shall he receive of the Lord, whether he be bond or free.

Ephesians 6:8

Finally, brethren, whatsoever things are true, whatsoever things are honest, whatsoever things are just, whatsoever things are pure, whatsoever things are lovely, whatsoever things are of good report; if there be any virtue, and if there be any praise, think on these things.

Philippians 4:8

When You Have Spent Money Unwisely

If my people, which are called by my name, shall humble themselves, and pray, and seek my face, and turn from their wicked ways; then will I hear from heaven, and will forgive their sin, and will heal their land.

2 Chronicles 7:14

Without counsel purposes are disappointed: but in the multitude of counsellors they are established.

Proverbs 15:22

Seest thou a man diligent in his business? he shall stand before kings; he shall not stand before mean men.

Proverbs 22:29

And I will restore to you the years that the locust hath eaten, the cankerworm, and the caterpillar, and the palmerworm, my great army which I sent among you.

And ye shall eat in plenty, and be satisfied, and praise the name of the LORD your God, that hath dealt wondrously with you: and my people shall never be ashamed.

Joel 2:25,26

And God is able to make all grace abound toward you; that ye, always having all sufficiency in all things, may abound to every good work:

2 Corinthians 9:8

For we have not an high priest which cannot be touched with the feeling of our infirmities; but was in all points tempted like as we are, yet without sin.

Hebrews 4:15

If we confess our sins, he is faithful and just to forgive us our sins, and to cleanse us from all unrighteousness.

1 John 1:9

When You Need Wisdom About Borrowing Money

For the LORD giveth wisdom: out of his mouth cometh knowledge and understanding.

Proverbs 2:6

Trust in the LORD with all thine heart; and lean not unto thine own understanding.

Proverbs 3:5

He becometh poor that dealeth with a slack hand: but the hand of the diligent maketh rich.

Proverbs 10:4

The hand of the diligent shall bear rule: but the slothful shall be under tribute.

Proverbs 12:24

The soul of the sluggard desireth, and hath nothing: but the soul of the diligent shall be made fat.

Proverbs 13:4

Without counsel purposes are disappointed: but in the multitude of counsellors they are established.

Proverbs 15:22

Love not sleep, lest thou come to poverty; open thine eyes, and thou shalt be satisfied with bread.

Proverbs 20:13

Seest thou a man diligent in his business? he shall stand before kings; he shall not stand before mean men.

Proverbs 22:29

Through wisdom is an house builded; and by understanding it is established:

Proverbs 24:3

He that tilleth his land shall have plenty of bread: but he that followeth after vain persons shall have poverty enough.

Proverbs 28:19

In the morning sow thy seed, and in the evening withhold not thine hand: for thou knowest not whether shall prosper, either this or that, or whether they both shall be alike good.

Ecclesiastes 11:6

Fear thou not; for I am with thee: be not dismayed; for I am thy God: I will strengthen thee; yea, I will help thee; yea, I will uphold thee with the right hand of my righteousness.

Isaiah 41:10

But seek ye first the kingdom of God, and his righteousness; and all these things shall be added unto you.

Matthew 6:33

Not slothful in business; fervent in spirit; serving the Lord;

Romans 12:11

When Tithing Seems Difficult

And blessed be the most high God, which hath delivered thine enemies into thy hand. And he gave him tithes of all.

Genesis 14:20

But thou shalt remember the LORD thy God: for it is he that giveth thee power to get wealth, that he may establish his covenant which he sware unto thy fathers, as it is this day.

Deuteronomy 8:18

Thou shalt truly tithe all the increase of thy seed, that the field bringeth forth year by year.

Deuteronomy 14:22

He that hath pity upon the poor lendeth unto the LORD; and that which he hath given will he pay him again.

Proverbs 19:17

He that giveth unto the poor shall not lack: but he that hideth his eyes shall have many a curse.

Proverbs 28:27

Bring ye all the tithes into the storehouse, that there may be meat in mine house, and prove me now herewith, saith the LORD of hosts, if I will not open you the windows of heaven, and pour you out a blessing, that there shall not be room enough to receive it.

And I will rebuke the devourer for your sakes, and he shall not destroy the fruits of your ground; neither shall your vine cast her fruit before the time in the field, saith the LORD of hosts.

Malachi 3:10,11

Give, and it shall be given unto you; good measure, pressed down, and shaken together, and running over, shall men give into your bosom. For with the same measure that ye mete withal it shall be measured to you again.

Luke 6:38

Upon the first day of the week let every one of you lay by him in store, as God hath prospered him, that there be no gatherings when I come.

1 Corinthians 16:2

But this I say, He which soweth sparingly shall reap also sparingly; and he which soweth bountifully shall reap also bountifully.

Every man according as he purposeth in his heart, so let him give; not grudgingly, or of necessity: for God loveth a cheerful giver.

And God is able to make all grace abound toward you; that ye, always having all sufficiency in all things, may abound to every good work:

2 Corinthians 9:6-8

But my God shall supply all your need according to his riches in glory by Christ Jesus.

Philippians 4:19

But whoso hath this world's good, and seeth his brother have need, and shutteth up his bowels of compassion from him, how dwelleth the love of God in him?

My little children, let us not love in word, neither in tongue; but in deed and in truth.

1 John 3:17,18

When Your Children Need To Learn the Blessing of Work

Be ye strong therefore, and let not your hands be weak: for your work shall be rewarded.

2 Chronicles 15:7

The soul of the sluggard desireth, and hath nothing: but the soul of the diligent shall be made fat.

Proverbs 13:4

The thoughts of the diligent tend only to plenteousness; but of every one that is hasty only to want.

Proverbs 21:5

Seest thou a man diligent in his business? he shall stand before kings; he shall not stand before mean men.

Proverbs 22:29

I must work the works of him that sent me, while it is day: the night cometh, when no man can work.

John 9:4

Now unto him that is able to do exceeding abundantly above all that we ask or think, according to the power that worketh in us,

Ephesians 3:20

I can do all things through Christ which strengtheneth me.

Philippians 4:13

Walk in wisdom toward them that are without, redeeming the time.

Colossians 4:5

If any of you lack wisdom, let him ask of God, that giveth to all men liberally, and upbraideth not; and it shall be given him.

James 1:5

Wherefore, beloved, seeing that ye look for such things, be diligent that ye may be found of him in peace, without spot, and blameless.

2 Peter 3:14

I know thy works: behold, I have set before thee an open door, and no man can shut it: for thou hast a little strength, and hast kept my word, and hast not denied my name.

Revelation 3:8

YOUR CHURCH

When Church Conflicts Disillusion You

O my God, I trust in thee: let me not be ashamed, let not mine enemies triumph over me.

Psalms 25:2

The LORD is my strength and my shield; my heart trusted in him, and I am helped: therefore my heart greatly rejoiceth; and with my song will I praise him.

Psalms 28:7

Therefore I will look unto the LORD; I will wait for the God of my salvation: my God will hear me.

Rejoice not against me, O mine enemy: when I fall, I shall arise; when I sit in darkness, the LORD shall be a light unto me.

Micah 7:7,8

Although the fig tree shall not blossom, neither shall fruit be in the vines; the labour of the olive shall fail, and the fields shall yield no meat; the flock shall be cut off from the fold, and there shall be no herd in the stalls:

Yet I will rejoice in the LORD, I will joy in the God of my salvation.

The LORD God is my strength, and he will make my feet like hinds' feet, and he will make me to walk upon mine high places. To the chief singer on my stringed instruments.

Habakkuk 3:17-19

For which cause we faint not; but though our outward man perish, yet the inward man is renewed day by day.

2 Corinthians 4:16

For we walk by faith, not by sight:

2 Corinthians 5:7

For the which cause I also suffer these things: nevertheless I am not ashamed: for I know whom I have believed, and am persuaded that he is able to keep that which I have committed unto him against that day.

2 Timothy 1:12

Wherefore lift up the hands which hang down, and the feeble knees;

And make straight paths for your feet, lest that which is lame be turned out of the way; but let it rather be healed.

Follow peace with all men, and holiness, without which no man shall see the Lord:

Looking diligently lest any man fail of the grace of God; lest any root of bitterness springing up trouble you, and thereby many be defiled;

Hebrews 12:12-15

When Someone Has Offended You

Thou shalt not avenge, nor bear any grudge against the children of thy people, but thou shalt love thy neighbour as thyself: I am the LORD.

Leviticus 19:18

O LORD my God, in thee do I put my trust: save me from all them that persecute me, and deliver me:

Psalms 7:1

And they that know thy name will put their trust in thee: for thou, LORD, hast not forsaken them that seek thee.

Psalms 9:10

Because he hath set his love upon me, therefore will I deliver him: I will set him on high, because he hath known my name.

He shall call upon me, and I will answer him: I will be with him in trouble; I will deliver him, and honour him.

Psalms 91:14,15

For the LORD will not cast off his people, neither will he forsake his inheritance.

Psalms 94:14

A fool's wrath is presently known: but a prudent man covereth shame.

Proverbs 12:16

Say not thou, I will recompense evil; but wait on the LORD, and he shall save thee.

Proverbs 20:22

But I say unto you, That whosoever is angry with his brother without a cause shall be in danger of the judgment: and whosoever shall say to his brother, Raca, shall be in danger of the council: but whosoever shall say, Thou fool, shall be in danger of hell fire.

Matthew 5:22

For if ye forgive men their trespasses, your heavenly Father will also forgive you:

Matthew 6:14

And if he trespass against thee seven times in a day, and seven times in a day turn again to thee, saying, I repent; thou shalt forgive him.

Luke 17:4

Recompense to no man evil for evil. Provide things honest in the sight of all men.

Romans 12:17

Charity suffereth long, and is kind; charity envieth not; charity vaunteth not itself, is not puffed up,

1 Corinthians 13:4

But now ye also put off all these; anger, wrath, malice, blasphemy, filthy communication out of your mouth.

Colossians 3:8

And the servant of the Lord must not strive; but be gentle unto all men, apt to teach, patient,

2 Timothy 2:24

Notwithstanding the Lord stood with me, and strengthened me; that by me the preaching might be fully known, and that all the Gentiles might hear: and I was delivered out of the mouth of the lion.

And the Lord shall deliver me from every evil work, and will preserve me unto his heavenly kingdom: to whom be glory for ever and ever. Amen.

2 Timothy 4:17,18

When You Are Asked To Accept Special Responsibilities

Ye are the salt of the earth: but if the salt have lost his savour, wherewith shall it be salted? it is thenceforth good for nothing, but to be cast out, and to be trodden under foot of men.

Ye are the light of the world. A city that is set on an hill cannot be hid.

Neither do men light a candle, and put it under a bushel, but on a candlestick; and it giveth light unto all that are in the house.

Let your light so shine before men, that they may see your good works, and glorify your Father which is in heaven.

Matthew 5:13-16

And whosoever shall give to drink unto one of these little ones a cup of cold water only in the name of a disciple, verily I say unto you, he shall in no wise lose his reward.

Matthew 10:42

Even as the Son of man came not to be ministered unto, but to minister, and to give his life a ransom for many.

Matthew 20:28

For I was an hungred, and ye gave me meat: I was thirsty, and ye gave me drink: I was a stranger, and ye took me in:

Naked, and ye clothed me: I was sick, and ye visited me: I was in prison, and ye came unto me.

Then shall the righteous answer him, saying, Lord, when saw we thee an hungred, and fed thee? or thirsty, and gave thee drink?

When saw we thee a stranger, and took thee in? or naked, and clothed thee?

Or when saw we thee sick, or in prison, and came unto thee?

And the King shall answer and say unto them, Verily I say unto you, Inasmuch as ye have done it unto one of the least of these my brethren, ye have done it unto me.

Matthew 25:35-40

And he said unto them, Go ye into all the world, and preach the gospel to every creature.

Mark 16:15

But ye shall receive power, after that the Holy Ghost is come upon you: and ye shall be witnesses unto me both in Jerusalem, and in all Judaea, and in Samaria, and unto the uttermost part of the earth.

Acts 1:8

Neglect not the gift that is in thee, which was given thee by prophecy, with the laying on of the hands of the presbytery.

1 Timothy 4:14

When You Feel Unqualified for a Church Position

And Caleb stilled the people before Moses, and said, Let us go up at once, and possess it; for we are well able to overcome it.

Numbers 13:30

But ye shall receive power, after that the Holy Ghost is come upon you: and ye shall be witnesses unto me both in Jerusalem, and in all Judaea, and in Samaria, and unto the uttermost part of the earth.

Acts 1:8

But God hath chosen the foolish things of the world to confound the wise; and God hath chosen the weak things of the world to confound the things which are mighty;

1 Corinthians 1:27

For to one is given by the Spirit the word of wisdom; to another the word of knowledge by the same Spirit;

1 Corinthians 12:8

And God is able to make all grace abound toward you; that ye, always having all sufficiency in all things, may abound to every good work:

2 Corinthians 9:8

And he said unto me, My grace is sufficient for thee: for my strength is made perfect in weakness. Most gladly therefore will I rather glory in my infirmities, that the power of Christ may rest upon me.

2 Corinthians 12:9

Now unto him that is able to do exceeding abundantly above all that we ask or think, according to the power that worketh in us,

Ephesians 3:20

I can do all things through Christ which strengtheneth me.

Philippians 4:13

Cast not away therefore your confidence, which hath great recompence of reward.

For ye have need of patience, that, after ye have done the will of God, ye might receive the promise.

Hebrews 10:35-36

Through faith also Sara herself received strength to conceive seed, and was delivered of a child when she was past age, because she judged him faithful who had promised.

Hebrews 11:11

If any of you lack wisdom, let him ask of God, that giveth to all men liberally, and upbraideth not; and it shall be given him.

James 1:5

When You Find It Difficult To Be the Spiritual Leader in Your Home

And that thou mayest tell in the ears of thy son, and of thy son's son, what things I have wrought in Egypt, and my signs which I have done among them; that ye may know how that I am the LORD.

Exodus 10:2

And thou shalt shew thy son in that day, saying, This is done because of that which the LORD did unto me when I came forth out of Egypt.

Exodus 13:8

Only take heed to thyself, and keep thy soul diligently, lest thou forget the things which thine eyes have seen, and lest they depart from thy heart all the days of thy life: but teach them thy sons, and thy sons' sons;

Deuteronomy 4:9

Counsel is mine, and sound wisdom: I am understanding; I have strength.

Proverbs 8:14

Fear thou not; for I am with thee: be not dismayed; for I am thy God: I will strengthen thee; yea, I will help thee; yea, I will uphold thee with the right hand of my righteousness.

Isaiah 41:10

The LORD God is my strength, and he will make my feet like hinds' feet, and he will make me to walk upon mine high places. To the chief singer on my stringed instruments.

Habakkuk 3:19

But ye shall receive power, after that the Holy Ghost is come upon you: and ye shall be witnesses unto me both in Jerusalem, and in all Judaea, and in Samaria, and unto the uttermost part of the earth.

Acts 1:8

Now unto him that is able to do exceeding abundantly above all that we ask or think, according to the power that worketh in us,

Ephesians 3:20

I can do all things through Christ which strengtheneth me.

Philippians 4:13

Strengthened with all might, according to his glorious power, unto all patience and longsuffering with joyfulness;

Colossians 1:11

Cast not away therefore your confidence, which hath great recompence of reward.

For ye have need of patience, that, after ye have done the will of God, ye might receive the promise.

Hebrews 10:35-36

When a Spiritual Mentor Fails

Keep me as the apple of the eye, hide me under the shadow of thy wings,

Psalms 17:8

For in the time of trouble he shall hide me in his pavilion: in the secret of his tabernacle shall he hide me; he shall set me up upon a rock.

Psalms 27:5

Even as the Son of man came not to be ministered unto, but to minister, and to give his life a ransom for many.

Matthew 20:28

But so shall it not be among you: but whosoever will be great among you, shall be your minister:

And whosoever of you will be the chiefest, shall be servant of all.

Mark 10:43,44

And he said, He that shewed mercy on him. Then said Jesus unto him, Go, and do thou likewise.

Luke 10:37

And the son said unto him, Father, I have sinned against heaven, and in thy sight, and am no more worthy to be called thy son.

But the father said to his servants, Bring forth the best robe, and put it on him; and put a ring on his hand, and shoes on his feet:

And bring hither the fatted calf, and kill it; and let us eat, and be merry:

For this my son was dead, and is alive again; he was lost, and is found. And they began to be merry.

Luke 15:21-24

Now the God of patience and consolation grant you to be likeminded one toward another according to Christ Jesus:

That ye may with one mind and one mouth glorify God, even the Father of our Lord Jesus Christ.

Wherefore receive ye one another, as Christ also received us to the glory of God.

Romans 15:5-7

Moreover it is required in stewards, that a man be found faithful.

1 Corinthians 4:2

Therefore, my beloved brethren, be ye stedfast, unmoveable, always abounding in the work of the Lord, forasmuch as ye know that your labour is not in vain in the Lord.

1 Corinthians 15:58

Brethren, if a man be overtaken in a fault, ye which are spiritual, restore such an one in the spirit of meekness; considering thyself, lest thou also be tempted.

Bear ye one another's burdens, and so fulfil the law of Christ.

As we have therefore opportunity, let us do good unto all men, especially unto them who are of the household of faith.

Galatians 6:1,2,10

Be ye therefore followers of God, as dear children;

And walk in love, as Christ also hath loved us, and hath given himself for us an offering and a sacrifice to God for a sweetsmelling savour.

Ephesians 5:1,2

Servants, be obedient to them that are your masters according to the flesh, with fear and trembling, in singleness of your heart, as unto Christ;

With good will doing service, as to the Lord, and not to men:

Ephesians 6:5,7

Forbearing one another, and forgiving one another, if any man have a quarrel against any: even as Christ forgave you, so also do ye.

Servants, obey in all things your masters according to the flesh; not with eyeservice, as menpleasers; but in singleness of heart, fearing God:

Colossians 3:13,22

Looking unto Jesus the author and finisher of our faith; who for the joy that was set before him endured the cross, despising the shame, and is set down at the right hand of the throne of God.

For consider him that endured such contradiction of sinners against himself, lest ye be wearied and faint in your minds.

Hebrews 12:2,3

For even hereunto were ye called: because Christ also suffered for us, leaving us an example, that ye should follow his steps:

1 Peter 2:21

If we confess our sins, he is faithful and just to forgive us our sins, and to cleanse us from all unrighteousness.

1 John 1:9

For all that is in the world, the lust of the flesh, and the lust of the eyes, and the pride of life, is not of the Father, but is of the world.

1 John 2:16

Hereby perceive we the love of God, because he laid down his life for us: and we ought to lay down our lives for the brethren.

1 John 3:16

As many as I love, I rebuke and chasten: be zealous therefore, and repent.

Revelation 3:19

YOUR PERSONAL NEEDS

When You Need Personal Motivation

There shall no man be able to stand before you: for the LORD your God shall lay the fear of you and the dread of you upon all the land that ye shall tread upon, as he hath said unto you.

Deuteronomy 11:25

The LORD shall cause thine enemies that rise up against thee to be smitten before thy face: they shall come out against thee one way, and flee before thee seven ways.

Deuteronomy 28:7

Be strong and of a good courage, fear not, nor be afraid of them: for the LORD thy God, he it is that doth go with thee; he will not fail thee, nor forsake thee.

Deuteronomy 31:6

Be strong and of a good courage: for unto this people shalt thou divide for an inheritance the land, which I sware unto their fathers to give them.

Joshua 1:6

For the LORD hath driven out from before you great nations and strong: but as for you, no man hath been able to stand before you unto this day.

Joshua 23:9

David encouraged himself in the LORD his God.

1 Samuel 30:6b

And he answered, Fear not: for they that be with us are more than they that be with them.

2 Kings 6:16

The spirit of the Lord GOD is upon me; because the LORD hath anointed me to preach good tidings unto the meek; he hath sent me to bind up the brokenhearted, to proclaim liberty to the captives, and the opening of the prison to them that are bound;

Isaiah 61:1

And they that be wise shall shine as the

brightness of the firmament; and they that turn many to righteousness as the stars for ever and ever.

Daniel 12:3

Ask, and it shall be given you; seek, and ye shall find; knock, and it shall be opened unto you:

For every one that asketh receiveth; and he that seeketh findeth; and to him that knocketh it shall be opened.

Matthew 7:7,8

And I say also unto thee, That thou art Peter, and upon this rock I will build my church; and the gates of hell shall not prevail against it.

And I will give unto thee the keys of the kingdom of heaven: and whatsoever thou shalt bind on earth shall be bound in heaven: and whatsoever thou shalt loose on earth shall be loosed in heaven.

Matthew 16:18,19

And ye shall know the truth, and the truth shall make you free. If the Son therefore shall make you free, ye shall be free indeed.

John 8:32,36

Verily, verily, I say unto you, He that believeth on me, the works that I do shall he do also; and greater works than these shall he do; because I go unto my Father.

John 14:12

But ye shall receive power, after that the Holy Ghost is come upon you: and ye shall be witnesses unto me both in Jerusalem, and in all Judaea, and in Samaria, and unto the uttermost part of the earth.

Acts 1:8

For the weapons of our warfare are not carnal, but mighty through God to the pulling down of strong holds;

2 Corinthians 10:4

Wherefore he saith, Awake thou that sleepest, and arise from the dead, and Christ shall give thee light.

Ephesians 5:14

I can do all things through Christ which strengtheneth me.

Philippians 4:13

Strengthened with all might, according to his glorious power, unto all patience and longsuffering with joyfulness;

Colossians 1:11

Walk in wisdom toward them that are without, redeeming the time.

Colossians 4:5

Meditate upon these things; give thyself wholly to them; that thy profiting may appear to all.

1 Timothy 4:15

Ye are of God, little children, and have overcome them: because greater is he that is in you, than he that is in the world.

Herein is our love made perfect, that we may have boldness in the day of judgment: because as he is, so are we in this world.

1 John 4:4,17

Beloved, I wish above all things that thou mayest prosper and be in health, even as thy soul prospereth.

3 John 1:2

When You Need Inner Peace

I will both lay me down in peace, and sleep: for thou, LORD, only makest me dwell in safety.

Psalms 4:8

What man is he that feareth the LORD? him shall he teach in the way that he shall choose.

His soul shall dwell at ease; and his seed shall inherit the earth.

Psalms 25:12,13

Thou wilt keep him in perfect peace, whose mind is stayed on thee: because he trusteth in thee.

LORD, thou wilt ordain peace for us: for thou also hast wrought all our works in us.

Isaiah 26:3,12

For ye shall go out with joy, and be led forth with peace: the mountains and the hills shall break forth before you into singing, and all the trees of the field shall clap their hands.

Isaiah 55:12

He shall enter into peace: they shall rest in their beds, each one walking in his uprightness.

Isaiah 57:2

Peace I leave with you, my peace I give unto you: not as the world giveth, give I unto you. Let not your heart be troubled, neither let it be afraid.

John 14:27

These things I have spoken unto you, that in me ye might have peace. In the world ye shall have tribulation: but be of good cheer; I have overcome the world.

John 16:33

Therefore being justified by faith, we have peace with God through our Lord Jesus Christ:

Romans 5:1

For to be carnally minded is death; but to be spiritually minded is life and peace.

Romans 8:6

Now the God of hope fill you with all joy and peace in believing, that ye may abound in hope, through the power of the Holy Ghost.

Romans 15:13

Finally, brethren, farewell. Be perfect, be of good comfort, be of one mind, live in peace; and the God of love and peace shall be with you.

2 Corinthians 13:11

Grace be to you and peace from God the Father, and from our Lord Jesus Christ,

Galatians 1:3

But the fruit of the Spirit is love, joy, peace, longsuffering, gentleness, goodness, faith,

Galatians 5:22

For he is our peace, who hath made both one, and hath broken down the middle wall of partition between us;

Ephesians 2:14

Be careful for nothing; but in every thing by prayer and supplication with thanksgiving let your requests be made known unto God.

And the peace of God, which passeth all understanding, shall keep your hearts and minds through Christ Jesus.

Those things, which ye have both learned, and received, and heard, and seen in me, do: and the God of peace shall be with you.

Philippians 4:6,7,9

And let the peace of God rule in your hearts, to the which also ye are called in one body; and be ye thankful.

Colossians 3:15

Now the Lord of peace himself give you peace always by all means. The Lord be with you all.

2 Thessalonians 3:16

But the wisdom that is from above is first pure, then peaceable, gentle, and easy to be intreated, full of mercy and good fruits, without partiality, and without hypocrisy.

And the fruit of righteousness is sown in peace of them that make peace.

James 3:17,18

When You Need To Forgive

But I say unto you, Love your enemies, bless them that curse you, do good to them that hate you, and pray for them which despitefully use you, and persecute you;

Matthew 5:44

And forgive us our debts, as we forgive our debtors.

For if ye forgive men their trespasses, your heavenly Father will also forgive you:

But if ye forgive not men their trespasses, neither will your Father forgive your trespasses.

Matthew 6:12-15

Then came Peter to him, and said, Lord, how oft shall my brother sin against me, and I forgive him? till seven times?

Matthew 18:21

Jesus saith unto him, "I say not unto thee, Until seven times: but, Until seventy times seven."

Matthew 18:22

And when ye stand praying, forgive, if ye have ought against any: that your Father also which is in heaven may forgive you your trespasses.

Mark 11:25

Take heed to yourselves: If thy brother trespass against thee, rebuke him; and if he repent, forgive him.

And if he trespass against thee seven times in a day, and seven times in a day turn again to thee, saying, I repent; thou shalt forgive him.

Luke 17:3,4

Whose soever sins ye remit, they are remitted unto them; and whose soever sins ye retain, they are retained.

John 20:23

Bless them which persecute you: bless, and curse not.

Be not overcome of evil, but overcome evil with good.

Romans 12:14,21

And be ye kind one to another, tenderhearted, forgiving one another, even as God for Christ's sake hath forgiven you.

Ephesians 4:32

Forbearing one another, and forgiving one another, if any man have a quarrel against any: even as Christ forgave you, so also do ye.

Colossians 3:13

Not rendering evil for evil, or railing for railing: but contrariwise blessing; knowing that ye are thereunto called, that ye should inherit a blessing.

1 Peter 3:9

When You Need To Apologize

That then the LORD thy God will turn thy captivity, and have compassion upon thee, and will return and gather thee from all the nations, whither the LORD thy God hath scattered thee.

Deuteronomy 30:3

If my people, which are called by my name, shall humble themselves, and pray, and seek my face, and turn from their wicked ways; then will I hear from heaven, and will forgive their sin, and will heal their land.

2 Chronicles 7:14

Cast thy burden upon the LORD, and he shall sustain thee: he shall never suffer the righteous to be moved.

Psalms 55:22

The LORD will perfect that which concerneth me: thy mercy, O LORD, endureth for ever: forsake not the works of thine own hands.

Psalms 138:8

Fear thou not; for I am with thee: be not dismayed; for I am thy God: I will strengthen thee; yea, I will help thee; yea, I will uphold thee with the right hand of my righteousness.

Isaiah 41:10

And I will restore to you the years that the locust hath eaten, the cankerworm, and the caterpillar, and the palmerworm, my great army which I sent among you.

Joel 2:25

And we know that all things work together for good to them that love God, to them who are the called according to his purpose.

Romans 8:28

For we walk by faith, not by sight:
2 Corinthians 5:7

Brethren, if a man be overtaken in a fault, ye which are spiritual, restore such an one in the spirit of meekness; considering thyself, lest thou also be tempted.

Bear ye one another's burdens, and so fulfil the law of Christ.
Galatians 6:1-2

Let nothing be done through strife or vainglory; but in lowliness of mind let each esteem other better than themselves.
Philippians 2:3

Brethren, I count not myself to have apprehended: but this one thing I do, forgetting those things which are behind, and reaching forth unto those things which are before,

I press toward the mark for the prize of the high calling of God in Christ Jesus.
Philippians 3:13-14

Let us hold fast the profession of our faith without wavering; for he is faithful that promised;
Hebrews 10:23

But without faith it is impossible to please him: for he that cometh to God must believe that he is, and that he is a rewarder of them that diligently seek him.

Hebrews 11:6

That the trial of your faith, being much more precious than of gold that perisheth, though it be tried with fire, might be found unto praise and honour and glory at the appearing of Jesus Christ:

1 Peter 1:7

But ye are a chosen generation, a royal priesthood, an holy nation, a peculiar people; that ye should shew forth the praises of him who hath called you out of darkness into his marvellous light:

1 Peter 2:9

Casting all your care upon him; for he careth for you.

1 Peter 5:7

When You Need Physical Healing

My son, attend to my words; incline thine ear unto my sayings.

Let them not depart from thine eyes; keep them in the midst of thine heart.

For they are life unto those that find them, and health to all their flesh.

Proverbs 4:20-22

A merry heart doeth good like a medicine: but a broken spirit drieth the bones.

Proverbs 17:22

Surely he hath borne our griefs, and carried our sorrows: yet we did esteem him stricken, smitten of God, and afflicted.

But he was wounded for our transgressions, he was bruised for our iniquities: the chastisement of our peace was upon him; and with his stripes we are healed.

Isaiah 53:4,5

For I will restore health unto thee, and I will heal thee of thy wounds, saith the LORD;

Jeremiah 30:17a

And Jesus saith unto him, I will come and heal him.

Matthew 8:7

And when the woman saw that she was not hid, she came trembling, and falling down before him, she declared unto him before all the people for what cause she had touched him, and how she was healed immediately.

And, behold, there was a woman which had a spirit of infirmity eighteen years, and was bowed together, and could in no wise lift up herself.

And when Jesus saw her, he called her to him, and said unto her, Woman, thou art loosed from thine infirmity.

Luke 8:45-47

Jesus Christ the same yesterday, and to day, and for ever.

Hebrews 13:8

Is any among you afflicted? let him pray. Is any merry? let him sing psalms.

Is any sick among you? let him call for the elders of the church; and let them pray over him, anointing him with oil in the name of the Lord:

And the prayer of faith shall save the sick, and the Lord shall raise him up; and if he have committed sins, they shall be forgiven him.

Confess your faults one to another, and pray one for another, that ye may be healed. The effectual fervent prayer of a righteous man availeth much.

James 5:13-16

Beloved, I wish above all things that thou mayest prosper and be in health, even as thy soul prospereth.

3 John 1:2

When You Need Wisdom

In that night did God appear unto Solomon, and said unto him, Ask what I shall give thee.

And Solomon said unto God, Thou hast shewed great mercy unto David my father, and hast made me to reign in his stead.

Now, O LORD God, let thy promise unto David my father be established: for thou hast made me king over a people like the dust of the earth in multitude.

Give me now wisdom and knowledge, that I may go out and come in before this people: for who can judge this thy people, that is so great?

And God said to Solomon, Because this was in thine heart, and thou hast not asked riches, wealth, or honour, nor the life of thine enemies, neither yet hast asked long life; but hast asked wisdom and knowledge for thyself, that thou mayest judge my people, over whom I have made thee king:

Wisdom and knowledge is granted unto thee; and I will give thee riches, and wealth, and honour, such as none of the kings have had that have been before thee, neither shall there any after thee have the like.

2 Chronicles 1:7-12

For the LORD giveth wisdom: out of his mouth cometh knowledge and understanding.

He layeth up sound wisdom for the righteous: he is a buckler to them that walk uprightly.

Proverbs 2:6,7

Trust in the LORD with all thine heart; and lean not unto thine own understanding.

In all thy ways acknowledge him, and he shall direct thy paths.

Proverbs 3:5,6

Wisdom is the principal thing; therefore get wisdom: and with all thy getting get understanding.

Exalt her, and she shall promote thee: she shall bring thee to honour, when thou dost embrace her.

Proverbs 4:7,8

Whoso loveth instruction loveth knowledge: but he that hateth reproof is brutish.

Proverbs 12:1

He that handleth a matter wisely shall find good: and whoso trusteth in the LORD, happy is he.

The wise in heart shall be called prudent: and the sweetness of the lips increaseth learning.

Understanding is a wellspring of life unto him that hath it: but the instruction of fools is folly.

The heart of the wise teacheth his mouth, and addeth learning to his lips.

Proverbs 16:20-23

Through wisdom is an house builded; and by understanding it is established:

And by knowledge shall the chambers be filled with all precious and pleasant riches.

Proverbs 24:3,4

My son, be wise, and make my heart glad, that I may answer him that reproacheth me.

Proverbs 27:11

For I will give you a mouth and wisdom, which all your adversaries shall not be able to gainsay nor resist.

Luke 21:15

Howbeit when he, the Spirit of truth, is come, he will guide you into all truth: for he shall not speak of himself; but whatsoever he shall hear, that shall he speak: and he will shew you things to come.

He shall glorify me: for he shall receive of mine, and shall shew it unto you.

John 16:13,14

For to one is given by the Spirit the word of wisdom; to another the word of knowledge by the same Spirit;

1 Corinthians 12:8

Cease not to give thanks for you, making mention of you in my prayers;

That the God of our Lord Jesus Christ, the Father of glory, may give unto you the spirit of wisdom and revelation in the knowledge of him:

The eyes of your understanding being enlightened; that ye may know what is the hope of his calling, and what the riches of the glory of his inheritance in the saints,

Ephesians 1:16-18

For this cause we also, since the day we heard it, do not cease to pray for you, and to desire that ye might be filled with the knowledge of his will in all wisdom and spiritual understanding;

That ye might walk worthy of the Lord unto all pleasing, being fruitful in every good work, and increasing in the knowledge of God;

Colossians 1:9,10

For God hath not given us the spirit of fear; but of power, and of love, and of a sound mind.

2 Timothy 1:7

If any of you lack wisdom, let him ask of God, that giveth to all men liberally, and upbraideth not; and it shall be given him.

James 1:5

When You Fail To Meet Your Personal Expectations

And he said, Come. And when Peter was come down out of the ship, he walked on the water, to go to Jesus.

But when he saw the wind boisterous, he was afraid; and beginning to sink, he cried, saying, Lord, save me.

And immediately Jesus stretched forth his hand, and caught him, and said unto him, O thou of little faith, wherefore didst thou doubt?

Matthew 14:29-31

Jesus said unto him, If thou canst believe, all things are possible to him that believeth.

Mark 9:23

And John calling unto him two of his disciples sent them to Jesus, saying, Art thou he that should come? or look we for another?

When the men were come unto him, they said, John Baptist hath sent us unto thee, saying, Art thou he that should come? or look we for another?

And in that same hour he cured many of their infirmities and plagues, and of evil spirits; and unto many that were blind he gave sight.

Then Jesus answering said unto them, Go your way, and tell John what things ye have seen and heard; how that the blind see, the lame walk, the lepers are cleansed, the deaf hear, the dead are raised, to the poor the gospel is preached.

And blessed is he, whosoever shall not be offended in me.

Luke 7:19-23

Therefore, my beloved brethren, be ye stedfast, unmoveable, always abounding in the work of the Lord, forasmuch as ye know that your labour is not in vain in the Lord.

1 Corinthians 15:58

And let us not be weary in well doing: for in due season we shall reap, if we faint not.

Galatians 6:9

For ye have need of patience, that, after ye have done the will of God, ye might receive the promise.

Now the just shall live by faith: but if any man draw back, my soul shall have no pleasure in him.

Hebrews 10:36,38

The Lord is not slack concerning his promise, as some men count slackness; but is longsuffering to us-ward, not willing that any should perish, but that all should come to repentance.

2 Peter 3:9

When You Feel Incapable of Achieving Your Goals and Dreams

I will instruct thee and teach thee in the way which thou shalt go: I will guide thee with mine eye.

Psalms 32:8

For with thee is the fountain of life: in thy light shall we see light.

Psalms 36:9

The LORD will perfect that which concerneth me: thy mercy, O LORD, endureth for ever: forsake not the works of thine own hands.

Psalms 138:8

A wise man will hear, and will increase learning; and a man of understanding shall attain unto wise counsels:

Proverbs 1:5

Wisdom is the principal thing; therefore get wisdom: and with all thy getting get understanding.

Proverbs 4:7

Exalt her, and she shall promote thee: she shall bring thee to honour, when thou dost embrace her.

Proverbs 4:8

That I may cause those that love me to inherit substance; and I will fill their treasures.

Proverbs 8:21

The thoughts of the righteous are right: but the counsels of the wicked are deceit.

Proverbs 12:5

So shall the knowledge of wisdom be unto thy soul: when thou hast found it, then there shall be a reward, and thy expectation shall not be cut off.

Proverbs 24:14

Behold, the former things are come to pass, and new things do I declare: before they spring forth I tell you of them.

Isaiah 42:9

Remember ye not the former things, neither consider the things of old.

Behold, I will do a new thing; now it shall spring forth; shall ye not know it? I will even make a way in the wilderness, and rivers in the desert.

Isaiah 43:18,19

For I know the thoughts that I think toward you, saith the LORD, thoughts of peace, and not of evil, to give you an expected end.

Jeremiah 29:11

And the LORD answered me, and said, Write the vision, and make it plain upon tables, that he may run that readeth it.

For the vision is yet for an appointed time, but at the end it shall speak, and not lie: though it tarry, wait for it; because it will surely come, it will not tarry.

Habakkuk 2:2,3

The LORD God is my strength, and he will make my feet like hinds' feet, and he will make me to walk upon mine high places.

Habakkuk 3:19

Ask, and it shall be given you; seek, and ye shall find; knock, and it shall be opened unto you:

Matthew 7:7

Be careful for nothing; but in every thing by prayer and supplication with thanksgiving let your requests be made known unto God.

Philippians 4:6

When You Feel Lonely and Unappreciated

Yea, though I walk through the valley of the shadow of death, I will fear no evil: for thou art with me; thy rod and thy staff they comfort me.

Psalms 23:4

The LORD is nigh unto them that are of a broken heart; and saveth such as be of a contrite spirit.

Psalms 34:18

I have been young, and now am old; yet have I not seen the righteous forsaken, nor his seed begging bread.

For the LORD loveth judgment, and forsaketh not his saints; they are preserved for ever: but the seed of the wicked shall be cut off.

Psalms 37:25,28

God is our refuge and strength, a very present help in trouble.

Psalms 46:1

He healeth the broken in heart, and bindeth up their wounds.

Psalms 147:3

Fear thou not; for I am with thee: be not dismayed; for I am thy God: I will strengthen thee; yea, I will help thee; yea, I will uphold thee with the right hand of my righteousness.

Isaiah 41:10

For the mountains shall depart, and the hills be removed; but my kindness shall not depart from thee, neither shall the covenant of my peace be removed, saith the LORD that hath mercy on thee.

Isaiah 54:10

But the very hairs of your head are all numbered.

Matthew 10:30

Teaching them to observe all things whatsoever I have commanded you: and, lo, I am with you alway, even unto the end of the world. Amen.

Matthew 28:20

Let not your heart be troubled: ye believe in God, believe also in me.

And I will pray the Father, and he shall give you another Comforter, that he may abide with you for ever;

Even the Spirit of truth; whom the world cannot receive, because it seeth him not, neither knoweth him: but ye know him; for he dwelleth with you, and shall be in you.

I will not leave you comfortless: I will come to you.

John 14:1,16-18

And the Lord shall deliver me from every evil work, and will preserve me unto his heavenly kingdom: to whom be glory for ever and ever. Amen.

2 Timothy 4:18

For we have not an high priest which cannot be touched with the feeling of our infirmities; but was in all points tempted like as we are, yet without sin.

Let us therefore come boldly unto the throne of grace, that we may obtain mercy, and find grace to help in time of need.

Hebrews 4:15,16

And be content with such things as ye have: for he hath said, I will never leave thee, nor forsake thee.

Hebrews 13:5b

Casting all your care upon him; for he careth for you.

1 Peter 5:7

When You Need to Overcome Anger

Be not hasty in thy spirit to be angry: for anger resteth in the bosom of fools.

Ecclesiastes 7:9

The Lord GOD hath given me the tongue of the learned, that I should know how to speak a word in season to him that is weary: he wakeneth morning by morning, he wakeneth mine ear to hear as the learned.

Isaiah 50:4

Blessed are the peacemakers: for they shall be called the children of God.

Matthew 5:9

For to be carnally minded is death; but to be spiritually minded is life and peace.

Romans 8:6

Now the works of the flesh are manifest, which are these; Adultery, fornication, uncleanness, lasciviousness,

Idolatry, witchcraft, hatred, variance, emulations, wrath, strife, seditions, heresies,

Envyings, murders, drunkenness, revellings, and such like: of the which I tell you before, as I have also told you in time past, that they which do such things shall not inherit the kingdom of God.

But the fruit of the Spirit is love, joy, peace, longsuffering, gentleness, goodness, faith,

Meekness, temperance: against such there is no law.

And they that are Christ's have crucified the flesh with the affections and lusts.

If we live in the Spirit, let us also walk in the Spirit.

Let us not be desirous of vain glory, provoking one another, envying one another.

Galatians 5:19-26

Be ye angry, and sin not: let not the sun go down upon your wrath:

Let all bitterness, and wrath, and anger, and clamour, and evil speaking, be put away from you, with all malice:

And be ye kind one to another, tender-hearted, forgiving one another, even as God for Christ's sake hath forgiven you.

Ephesians 4:26,31,32

Let nothing be done through strife or vainglory; but in lowliness of mind let each esteem other better than themselves.

Look not every man on his own things, but every man also on the things of others.

Philippians 2:3,4

Wherefore, my beloved brethren, let every man be swift to hear, slow to speak, slow to wrath:

For the wrath of man worketh not the righteousness of God.

James 1:19,20

When You Need To Overcome Resentment

Charity suffereth long, and is kind; charity envieth not; charity vaunteth not itself, is not puffed up,

Doth not behave itself unseemly, seeketh not her own, is not easily provoked, thinketh no evil;

1 Corinthians 13:4,5

For the weapons of our warfare are not carnal, but mighty through God to the pulling down of strong holds;

2 Corinthians 10:4

Let all bitterness, and wrath, and anger, and clamour, and evil speaking, be put away from you, with all malice:

Ephesians 4:31

Finally, my brethren, be strong in the Lord, and in the power of his might.

Ephesians 6:10

Finally, brethren, whatsoever things are true, whatsoever things are honest, whatsoever things are just, whatsoever things are pure, whatsoever things are lovely, whatsoever things are of good report; if there be any virtue, and if there be any praise, think on these things.

Philippians 4:8

Who is a wise man and endued with knowledge among you? let him shew out of a good conversation his works with meekness of wisdom.

For where envying and strife is, there is confusion and every evil work.

James 3:13,16

When You Need To Overcome Envy or Jealousy

Keep thy tongue from evil, and thy lips from speaking guile.

Psalms 34:13

Fret not thyself because of evildoers, neither be thou envious against the workers of iniquity.

Psalms 37:1

Envy thou not the oppressor, and choose none of his ways.

Proverbs 3:31

A sound heart is the life of the flesh: but envy the rottenness of the bones.

Proverbs 14:30

Death and life are in the power of the tongue: and they that love it shall eat the fruit thereof.

Proverbs 18:21

Be not thou envious against evil men, neither desire to be with them.

Proverbs 24:1

Set me as a seal upon thine heart, as a seal upon thine arm: for love is strong as death; jealousy is cruel as the grave: the coals thereof are coals of fire, which hath a most vehement flame.

Song of Solomon 8:6

Be ye therefore perfect, even as your Father which is in heaven is perfect.

Matthew 5:48

Judge not, that ye be not judged.

Matthew 7:1

Let us walk honestly, as in the day; not in rioting and drunkenness, not in chambering and wantonness, not in strife and envying.

Romans 13:13

For ye are yet carnal: for whereas there is among you envying, and strife, and divisions, are ye not carnal, and walk as men?

1 Corinthians 3:3

Charity suffereth long, and is kind; charity envieth not; charity vaunteth not itself, is not puffed up,

1 Corinthians 13:4

And they that are Christ's have crucified the flesh with the affections and lusts.

If we live in the Spirit, let us also walk in the Spirit.

Let us not be desirous of vain glory, provoking one another, envying one another.

Galatians 5:24-26

Let no corrupt communication proceed out of your mouth, but that which is good to the use of edifying, that it may minister grace unto the hearers.

Let all bitterness, and wrath, and anger, and clamour, and evil speaking, be put away from you, with all malice:

Ephesians 4:29,31

Wherefore laying aside all malice, and all guile, and hypocrisies, and envies, and all evil speakings,

As newborn babes, desire the sincere milk of the word, that ye may grow thereby:

1 Peter 2:1,2

Not rendering evil for evil, or railing for railing: but contrariwise blessing; knowing that ye are thereunto called, that ye should inherit a blessing.

For he that will love life, and see good days, let him refrain his tongue from evil, and his lips that they speak no guile:

1 Peter 3:9,10

But ye, beloved, building up yourselves on your most holy faith, praying in the Holy Ghost,

Jude 1:20

When You Feel Anxious About Your Advancing Age

And Moses was an hundred and twenty years old when he died: his eye was not dim, nor his natural force abated.

Deuteronomy 34:7

Surely goodness and mercy shall follow me all the days of my life: and I will dwell in the house of the LORD for ever.

Psalms 23:6

They shall still bring forth fruit in old age; they shall be fat and flourishing;

Psalms 92:14

For length of days, and long life, and peace, shall they add to thee.

Proverbs 3:2

He giveth power to the faint; and to them that have no might he increaseth strength.

Even the youths shall faint and be weary, and the young men shall utterly fall:

But they that wait upon the LORD shall renew their strength; they shall mount up with wings as eagles; they shall run, and not be weary; and they shall walk, and not faint.

Isaiah 40:29-31

Let your conversation be without covetousness; and be content with such things as ye have: for he hath said, I will never leave thee, nor forsake thee.

Hebrews 13:5

When You Feel Used

And they that know thy name will put their trust in thee: for thou, LORD, hast not forsaken them that seek thee.

Psalms 9:10

Many are the afflictions of the righteous: but the LORD delivereth him out of them all.

Psalms 34:19

Because he hath set his love upon me, therefore will I deliver him: I will set him on high, because he hath known my name.

He shall call upon me, and I will answer him: I will be with him in trouble; I will deliver him, and honour him.

Psalms 91:14,15

Trust in the LORD with all thine heart; and lean not unto thine own understanding.

In all thy ways acknowledge him, and he shall direct thy paths.

Proverbs 3:5,6

Fear thou not; for I am with thee: be not dismayed; for I am thy God: I will strengthen thee; yea, I will help thee; yea, I will uphold thee with the right hand of my righteousness.

Isaiah 41:10

Can a woman forget her sucking child, that she should not have compassion on the son of her womb? yea, they may forget, yet will I not forget thee.

Behold, I have graven thee upon the palms of my hands; thy walls are continually before me.

Isaiah 49:15,16

And, lo, I am with you alway, even unto the end of the world. Amen.

Matthew 28:20b

Behold, I give unto you power to tread on serpents and scorpions, and over all the power of the enemy: and nothing shall by any means hurt you.

Luke 10:19

What shall we then say to these things? If God be for us, who can be against us?

Romans 8:31

So that we may boldly say, The Lord is
my helper, and I will not fear what man shall
do unto me.

Hebrews 13:6

Casting all your care upon him; for he
careth for you.

1 Peter 5:7

And they overcame him by the blood of
the Lamb, and by the word of their testimony; and they loved not their lives unto
the death.

Revelation 12:11

When You Feel Depressed

For his anger endureth but a moment;
in his favour is life: weeping may endure for
a night, but joy cometh in the morning.

Psalms 30:5

The righteous cry, and the LORD
heareth, and delivereth them out of all their
troubles.

Psalms 34:17

I will praise thee with my whole heart:
before the gods will I sing praise unto thee.

Psalms 138:1

Happy is the man that findeth wisdom, and the man that getteth understanding.

Her ways are ways of pleasantness, and all her paths are peace.

She is a tree of life to them that lay hold upon her: and happy is every one that retaineth her.

Proverbs 3:13,17-18

The wilderness and the solitary place shall be glad for them; and the desert shall rejoice, and blossom as the rose.

And the ransomed of the LORD shall return, and come to Zion with songs and everlasting joy upon their heads: they shall obtain joy and gladness, and sorrow and sighing shall flee away.

Isaiah 35:1

But they that wait upon the LORD shall renew their strength; they shall mount up with wings as eagles; they shall run, and not be weary; and they shall walk, and not faint.

Isaiah 40:31

Fear thou not; for I am with thee: be not dismayed; for I am thy God: I will strengthen thee; yea, I will help thee; yea, I will uphold thee with the right hand of my righteousness.

Isaiah 41:10

When thou passest through the waters, I will be with thee; and through the rivers, they shall not overflow thee: when thou walkest through the fire, thou shalt not be burned; neither shall the flame kindle upon thee.

Isaiah 43:2

For the Lord GOD will help me; therefore shall I not be confounded: therefore have I set my face like a flint, and I know that I shall not be ashamed.

Isaiah 50:7

For I am persuaded, that neither death, nor life, nor angels, nor principalities, nor powers, nor things present, nor things to come,

Nor height, nor depth, nor any other creature, shall be able to separate us from the love of God, which is in Christ Jesus our Lord.

Romans 8:38,39

Blessed be God, even the Father of our Lord Jesus Christ, the Father of mercies, and the God of all comfort;

Who comforteth us in all our tribulation, that we may be able to comfort them which are in any trouble, by the comfort wherewith we ourselves are comforted of God.

2 Corinthians 1:3,4

Beloved, think it not strange concerning the fiery trial which is to try you, as though some strange thing happened unto you:

But rejoice, inasmuch as ye are partakers of Christ's sufferings; that, when his glory shall be revealed, ye may be glad also with exceeding joy.

1 Peter 4:12,13

When You Feel Sexual Temptation

But thou, O LORD, art a shield for me; my glory, and the lifter up of mine head.

Psalms 3:3

Let integrity and uprightness preserve me; for I wait on thee.

Psalms 25:21

Judge me, O LORD; for I have walked in mine integrity: I have trusted also in the LORD; therefore I shall not slide.

But as for me, I will walk in mine integrity: redeem me, and be merciful unto me.

Psalms 26:1,11

Be pleased, O LORD, to deliver me: O LORD, make haste to help me.

Let them be ashamed and confounded together that seek after my soul to destroy it; let them be driven backward and put to shame that wish me evil.

Psalms 40:13,14

It is better to trust in the LORD than to put confidence in man.

Psalms 118:8

Thy word have I hid in mine heart, that I might not sin against thee.

Psalms 119:11

For the LORD shall be thy confidence, and shall keep thy foot from being taken.

Proverbs 3:26

And lead us not into temptation, but deliver us from evil: For thine is the kingdom, and the power, and the glory, for ever. Amen.

Matthew 6:13

Watch and pray, that ye enter not into temptation: the spirit indeed is willing, but the flesh is weak.

Matthew 26:41

For sin shall not have dominion over you: for ye are not under the law, but under grace.

Romans 6:14

There hath no temptation taken you but such as is common to man: but God is faithful, who will not suffer you to be tempted above that ye are able; but will with the temptation also make a way to escape, that ye may be able to bear it.

1 Corinthians 10:13

And my temptation which was in my flesh ye despised not, nor rejected; but received me as an angel of God, even as Christ Jesus.

Galatians 4:14

That ye put off concerning the former conversation the old man, which is corrupt according to the deceitful lusts;

Ephesians 4:22

For in that he himself hath suffered being tempted, he is able to succour them that are tempted.

Hebrews 2:18

Let no man say when he is tempted, I am tempted of God: for God cannot be tempted with evil, neither tempteth he any man:

But every man is tempted, when he is drawn away of his own lust, and enticed.

James 1:13,14

Be sober, be vigilant; because your adversary the devil, as a roaring lion, walketh about, seeking whom he may devour:

Whom resist stedfast in the faith, knowing that the same afflictions are accomplished in your brethren that are in the world.

1 Peter 5:8,9

The Lord knoweth how to deliver the godly out of temptations, and to reserve the unjust unto the day of judgment to be punished:

2 Peter 2:9

Because thou hast kept the word of my patience, I also will keep thee from the hour of temptation, which shall come upon all the world, to try them that dwell upon the earth.

Revelation 3:10

When You Feel Guilty

A good man out of the good treasure of the heart bringeth forth good things: and an evil man out of the evil treasure bringeth forth evil things.

For by thy words thou shalt be justified, and by thy words thou shalt be condemned.

Matthew 12:35,37

Behold, I give unto you power to tread on serpents and scorpions, and over all the power of the enemy: and nothing shall by any means hurt you.

Luke 10:19

Let not your heart be troubled: ye believe in God, believe also in me.

John 14:1

God forbid: yea, let God be true, but every man a liar; as it is written, That thou mightest be justified in thy sayings, and mightest overcome when thou art judged.

Romans 3:4

We are troubled on every side, yet not distressed; we are perplexed, but not in despair;

Persecuted, but not forsaken; cast down, but not destroyed;

2 Corinthians 4:8,9

Above all, taking the shield of faith, wherewith ye shall be able to quench all the fiery darts of the wicked.

Ephesians 6:16

But the Lord is faithful, who shall stablish you, and keep you from evil.

2 Thessalonians 3:3

And the Lord shall deliver me from every evil work, and will preserve me unto his heavenly kingdom: to whom be glory for ever and ever. Amen.

2 Timothy 4:18